To the Pratt Family,

1974.

With love

Ruth.

Parents see Page 214

Science for Work and Play

Science for Here and Now

Science Far and Near

Science in Your Life

Science in Our World

Science for Today and Tomorrow

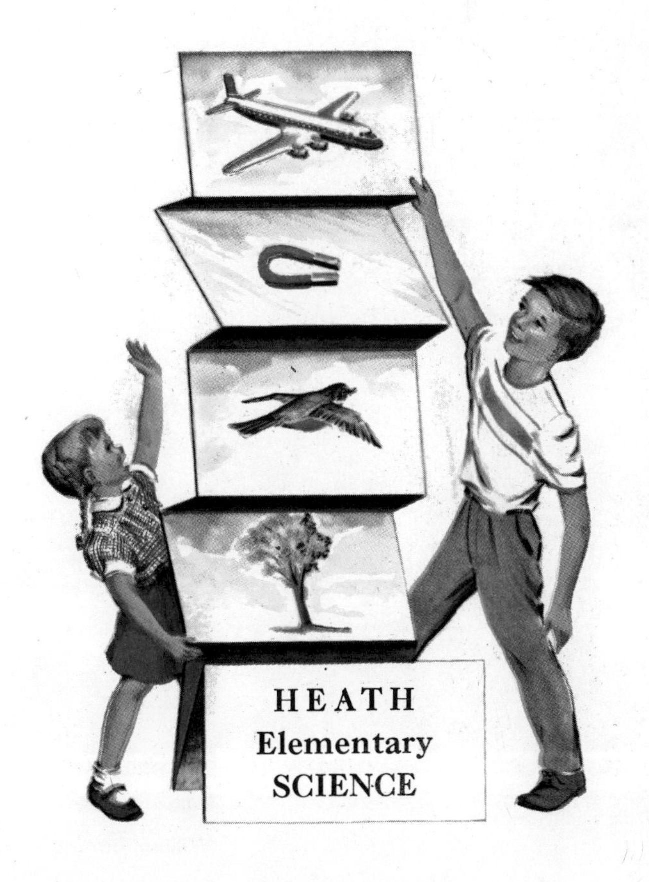

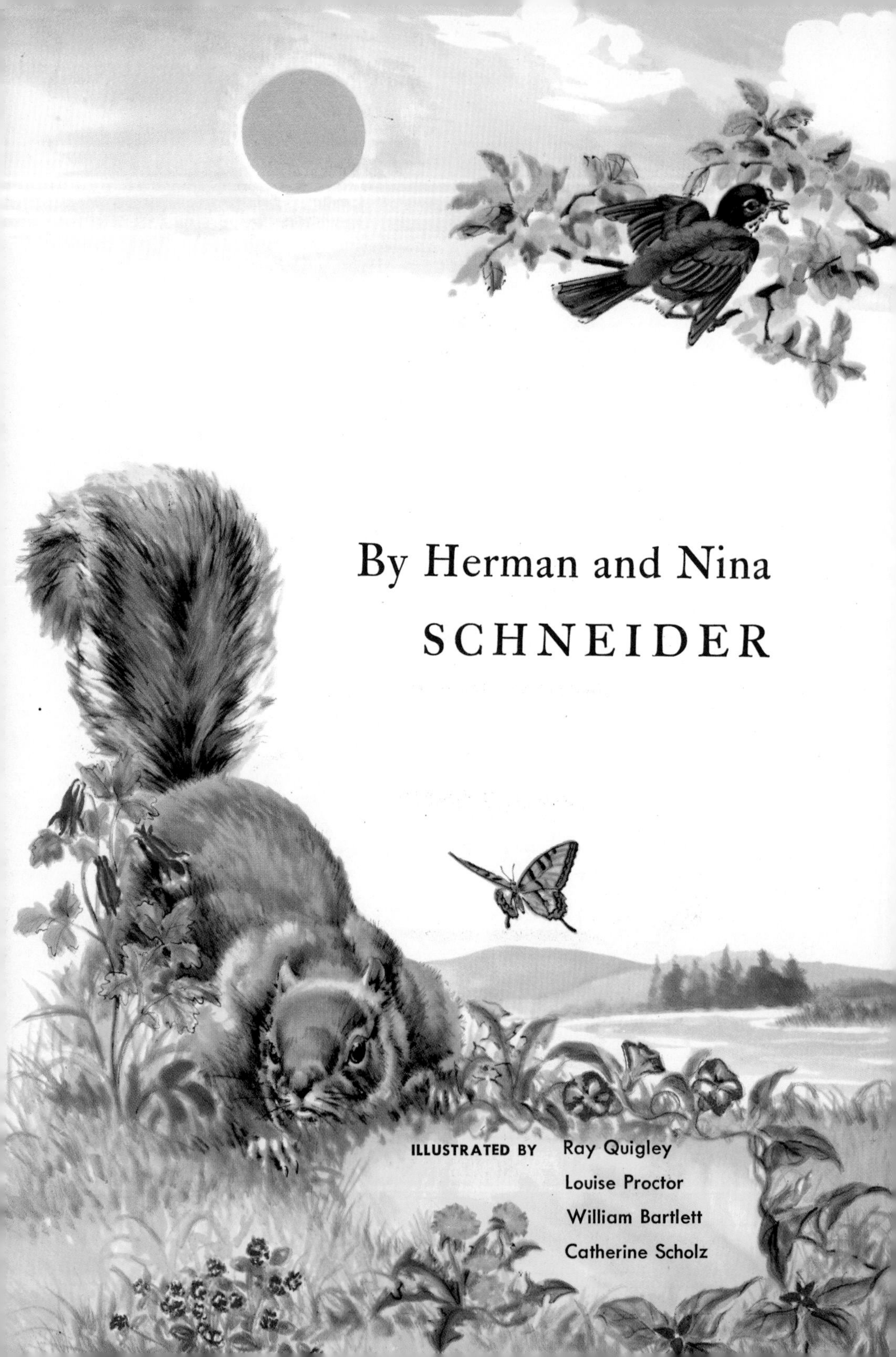

By Herman and Nina
SCHNEIDER

ILLUSTRATED BY Ray Quigley
Louise Proctor
William Bartlett
Catherine Scholz

SCIENCE for Here and Now

D. C. HEATH AND COMPANY

CONTENTS

YOUR DAY

Good morning!
Good morning to you!
The day is here.
Did you have a good sleep?
Did you like the ride?
Do you know that you had a ride?

You are still riding.
You ride while you wash.
You ride while you dress.
You ride while you eat.
Go out into the sun.
You are still riding.

The Earth Turns

You ride because the earth turns.
The earth is a big round ball that turns.
It turns all the time.
You cannot feel it turn.
It turns so very softly.
You ride on the softly turning earth.

Day and Night

The earth keeps turning
and turning.
You ride on a turning earth.
The big sun gives heat
and light to the turning earth.
You ride in the sunlight.
When you ride in the warm
sunlight, it is day.
The sun gives the light of day.

When you ride out of the sunlight, it is night.

It is dark night.

The earth keeps turning and turning.

The turning brings day and night, day and night.

It brings day and night all around the earth.

The sun is always shining.
The earth is always turning.
You cannot see the earth turning.
But you can see the globe turning.
You can see one side of the globe in the light.
This side is in sunlight.
It is day on the side where we live.

Now turn the globe.
Our side is away from the light now.
Our side is in the dark.
It is night on the side
where we live.
See day and night on the globe.
Every full turn is one day
and one night.

Turn, turn, turn like the earth.
Turn from dark night to morning.
See the day begin for you.
Keep turning as the earth keeps turning.
See the bright sunlight change to sunset.

Turn away from the sun,
into the night.
The night is not all dark.
Sometimes you can see
the stars shining.
Sometimes you can see the moon.
Turn in the soft light
of the stars and moon.
Turn from dark night to sunrise.
Begin another day.

Work and Play

Your day waits for you.
Ride into the new day.
Ride in the light of the sun.
Day is the time for work and play.
Work on the turning earth.
Play on the turning earth.
Ride on the turning earth
through the day.

Ride out of the sunlight into night.
What do we see in the night?
Sometimes we see the stars.
Sometimes clouds are in the way.
Sometimes we see the moon.
Sometimes the moon has gone away.
Sometimes we see the moon by day.

Sleep and Rest

After the day, night comes.
Night is the time for home and rest.
Night is the time for sleep and rest.
Sleep and rest on the turning earth.
Sleep and rest until the day comes.
The earth always turns.
The new day always comes.

Things to Talk About

1. Tell what makes night and day.
2. Which picture is right? Tell why.

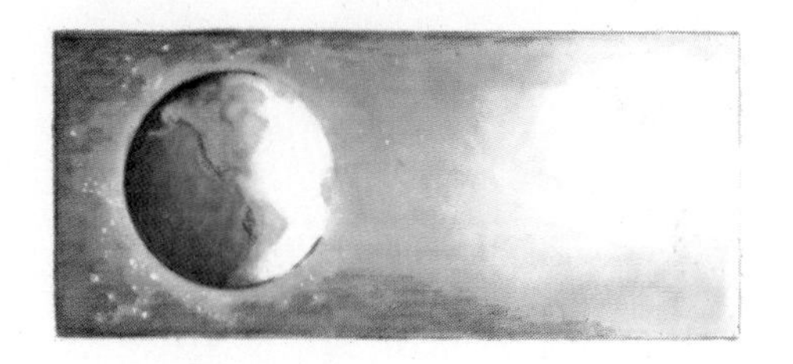

3. Talk about changes in the sky during the day and the night.
4. Talk about a trip to the moon.

Things to Do

1. Mark the sunrise and sunset sides of your room. Mark East and West.
2. Make a picture story about some night workers.
3. Draw a line around a spot of sunlight on the blackboard.
   Mark the spot of sunlight later.
   Is the spot of sunlight in the same place?
   Can you tell why?

Things to Find Out

1. Find the thing above that is round like the earth.
2. How much sleep do you need?
3. Can you see the moon on a rainy night?
4. Find out about moons made by man. What are they called?

DOING WORK

So many boxes!

So many heavy, heavy boxes!

The men are working hard.

It is hard work to carry heavy things.

Is there an easier way?

It is hard to carry the boxes.
It is easier to slide them.
It is hard to drag the heavy boxes.
It is easier to roll them.
Sliding and rolling make
the work easier.

How Rolling Helps

EXPERIMENT

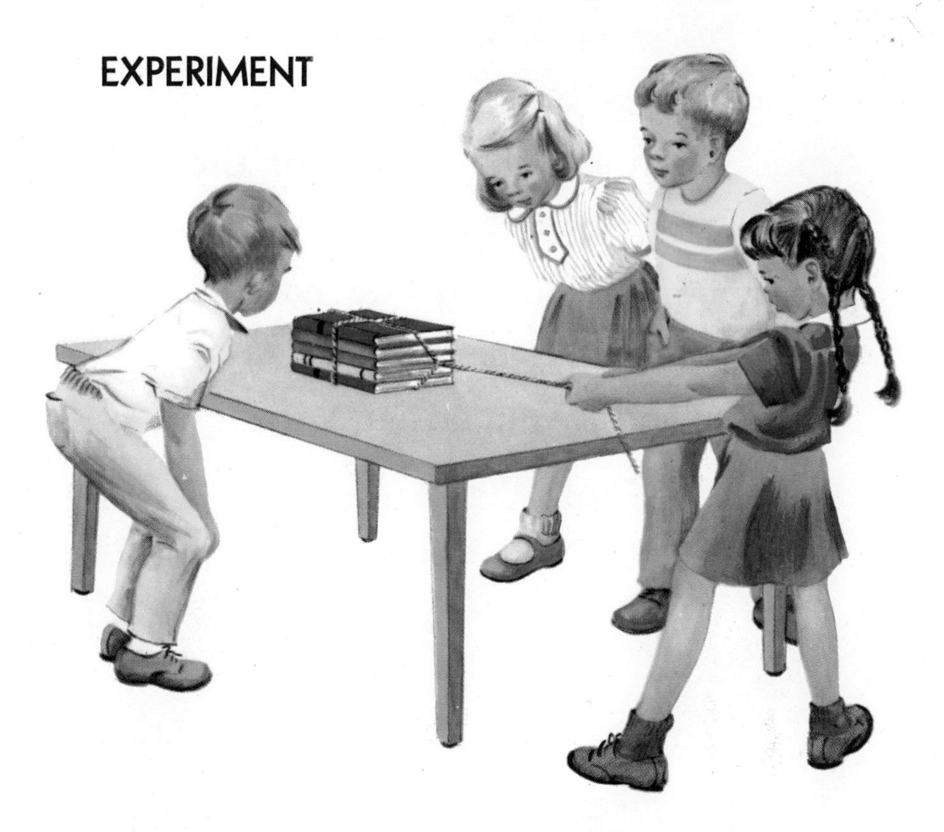

It is not easy to pull these books this way.

The books and the table rub on each other.

Is there an easier way to pull the books?

Here is an easier way
to pull the books.

Put some round things
under the books.

The round things do not drag
on the table.

The round things do not rub.

The round things roll.

Rolling is an easier way
to move something.

How Wheels Help

EXPERIMENT

See how wheels help.
Wheels are round like rollers.
They roll like rollers.
Rolling is easier than dragging.

How Ramps Help

EXPERIMENT

This is hard work.
It is too hard.
We cannot lift this heavy load.
Maybe there is an easier way.

Here is an easier way.

We make a ramp.

We slide the box up the ramp.

We do not have to lift the heavy box.

A ramp makes work easier.

Wheels and Ramps Make Work Easier

Men are building a house.
Many heavy things must be moved.
They must be moved up and moved down.
It is hard work to build a house.
What do the men use to make the work easier?

Wheels make work easier.
The men use wheels to help them.
Find the wheels they use.
Tell how they make work easier.

Ramps make work easier.
It is easier to move things on a ramp than to lift them.
The men use ramps to help them move things.
Find the ramps they use.
Tell how the wheels and ramps make work easier.

A Note Book About Ramps

We can make a note book.

We can put an experiment about ramps in our note book.

We tell these things about an experiment.

1. What we want to find out.
   Do ramps make work easier?
2. What we do.
   We try to lift a load.
   Then we slide the load up a ramp.
3. What we find out.
   We find that ramps make work easier.

Wheels and Ramps at School

The children are making a book.
It will show wheels and ramps
in their school.
Can you find wheels and ramps
in your school?

Things to Talk About

1. On your way to school you see people working.
   Tell about them.
   Tell about any wheels and ramps you see.

2. Which way is easier?
   Tell why.

3. Tell about some work mothers do at home.
   Tell about some work fathers do at home.
   Tell about some work you can do at home.

Things to Do

1. Plan a trip to a new building.
   Make pictures of things with wheels that can help take you there.

2. Start a class chart like this.

What we did	What we found out
	Rollers help.
	Wheels help.
	Ramps help.

Things to Find Out

1. Go to see the man who takes care of your school.
   Find out how wheels and ramps help him do his work.

2. Go to a building where people sell things.
   Find out about machines that help them.

3. Is there a building near your school where people make things?
   Find out what machines help them.

FALL BRINGS CHANGES

Look up! Look down! Look around!
Fall has come.
See it. Smell it.
Taste it. Feel it.
Hear it.
We can tell that fall is here.

Birds Fly Away

Do birds know that fall is here?
Do birds know that soon it will be cold?
The birds seem to know something.
Something about the fall seems to tell them to go.
Something tells them where to go.
The birds cannot tell us how they know.
But they seem to know.

Do you know the birds in the pictures?
They fly away from winter.
They fly to warmer places.
They fly away to sunny places.

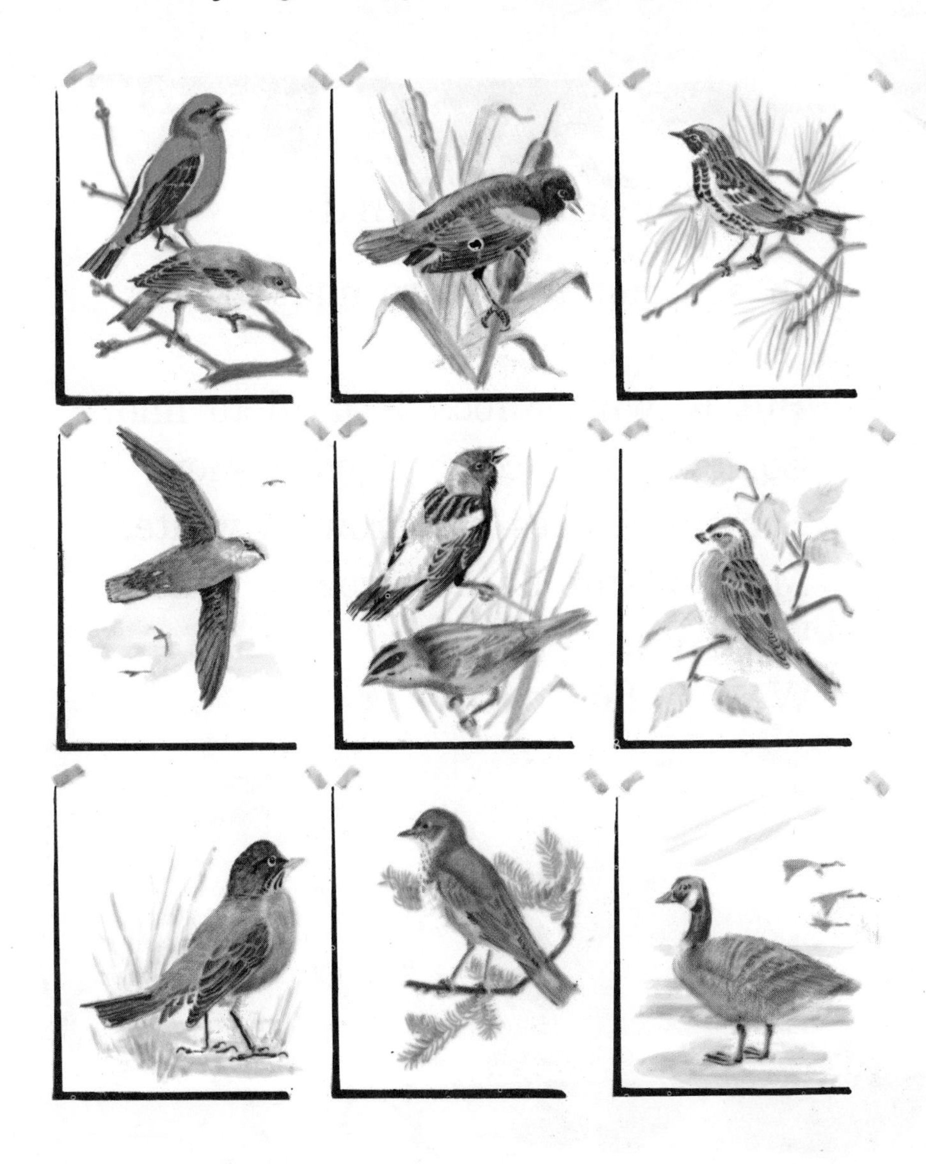

Food for Birds

In summer there are many kinds of food for birds.

But in winter food is hard to find.

Some of it is covered with snow.

Some of it does not grow in winter.

Many plants do not grow in winter.

Why not?

We can find out.

Plants and Cold

Here is how we can find out.

Put one plant in a cold place.
Put one plant in a warm place.

Leave them for a few days.
What has happened?
The plant in the cold did not grow.

Birds can fly away,
but plants must stay.

What happens to the plants
when the cold days come?

The leaves fall from many
of the plants.

Some plants do not live in winter.
But the seeds live.
The seeds fall to the ground.
They lie there a long time.
Then one day they begin to grow.
When do they begin to grow?
We can find out.

EXPERIMENT

Get some of these seeds.
Plant them in two boxes of wet soil.
Put one box in a warm place.
Put one box in a cold place.
Do some seeds grow when they are warm?
When will the seeds in the ground be warm?
What will warm them?

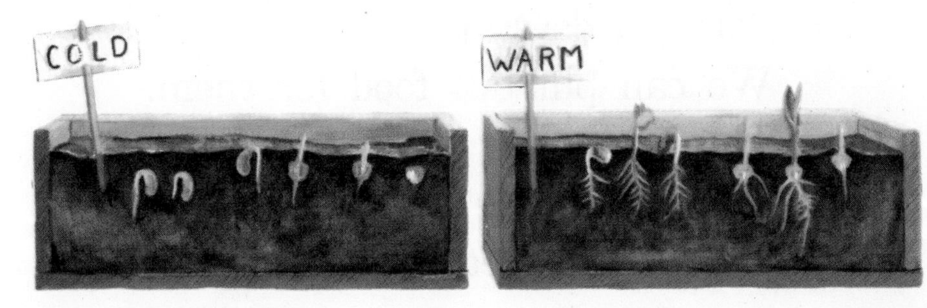

Feeding Birds in Winter

Many birds fly away.
Some birds stay.
We can put out food for them.
The birds may come to the food.
We like to see them.
We like to feed them.

Getting Food in Winter

Here are some birds!

Here they have the food they need.

People need food, too.
Do people fly away with the birds?
No! They can stay where they are.
How do people get their food in winter?

How Food Travels

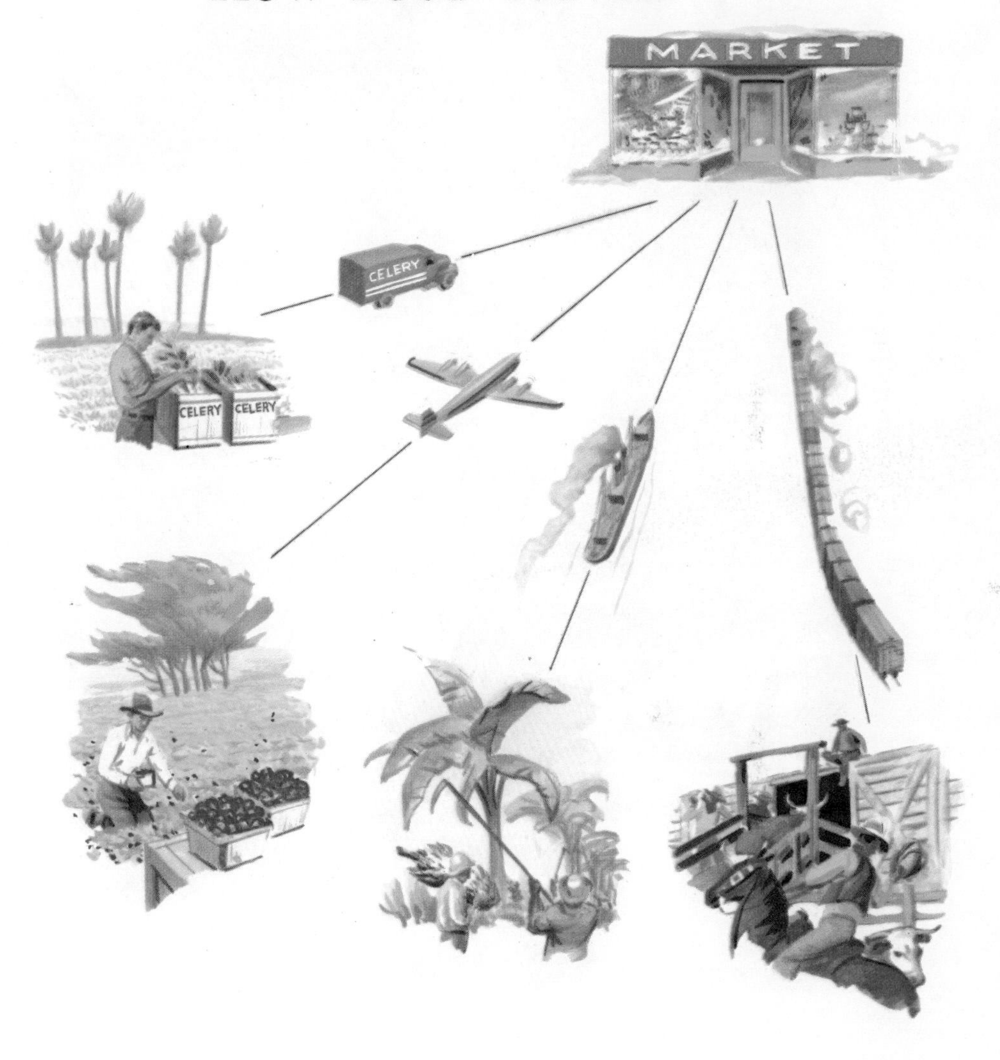

People do not have to go
to their food.
Their food comes to them.

Food comes to us in many ways.
Many people help to bring it.
People help each other.

Things to Talk About

1. How do we know it is fall?
   Tell about the weather.
   Tell how the plants look.
   Tell about the games you play.
   What clothing do you wear?

2. Tell about any birds you saw on your way to school.

3. Tell about some things a pet can learn.
   Tell about some things animals know by themselves.

4. Talk about why farmers plant seeds in the spring.

Things to Do

1. Plan a trip to a park or woods.
   Draw a picture of your trip.
   Make a little park or woods on the sand table.

2. Make a collection of leaves and seeds on your trip to the park or woods.
   Plant some of the seeds.
   See how many will grow.

3. Make a fall chart. Put fall things on it. Show things you hear, smell, taste, see, and feel.

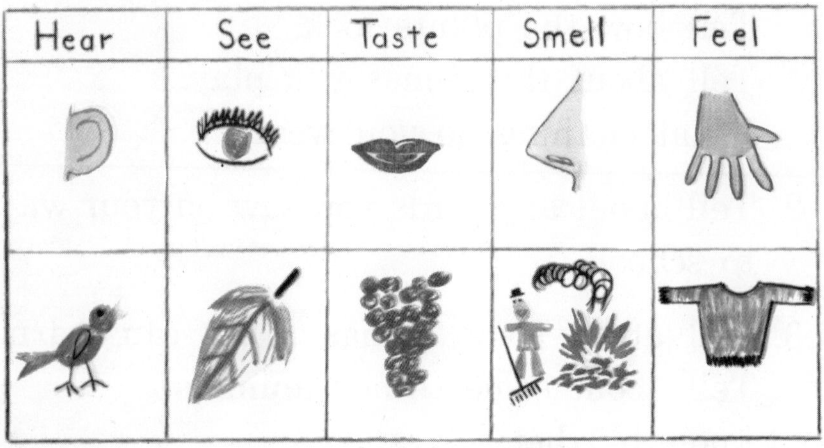

Hear	See	Taste	Smell	Feel

4. Make a picture story of a bean plant.

Things to Find Out

1. Find out about some birds in your neighborhood.
2. Find out how to feed birds in winter.
3. Tell what foods you ate yesterday. Find out where the foods you ate yesterday came from.
4. Find out how the foods you ate yesterday came to your town.

THE NEW BUILDING

Trucks, trucks, trucks!
Look at all the busy trucks.
What are the busy trucks bringing to the new building?
We can find out.
We can plan a trip to find out.

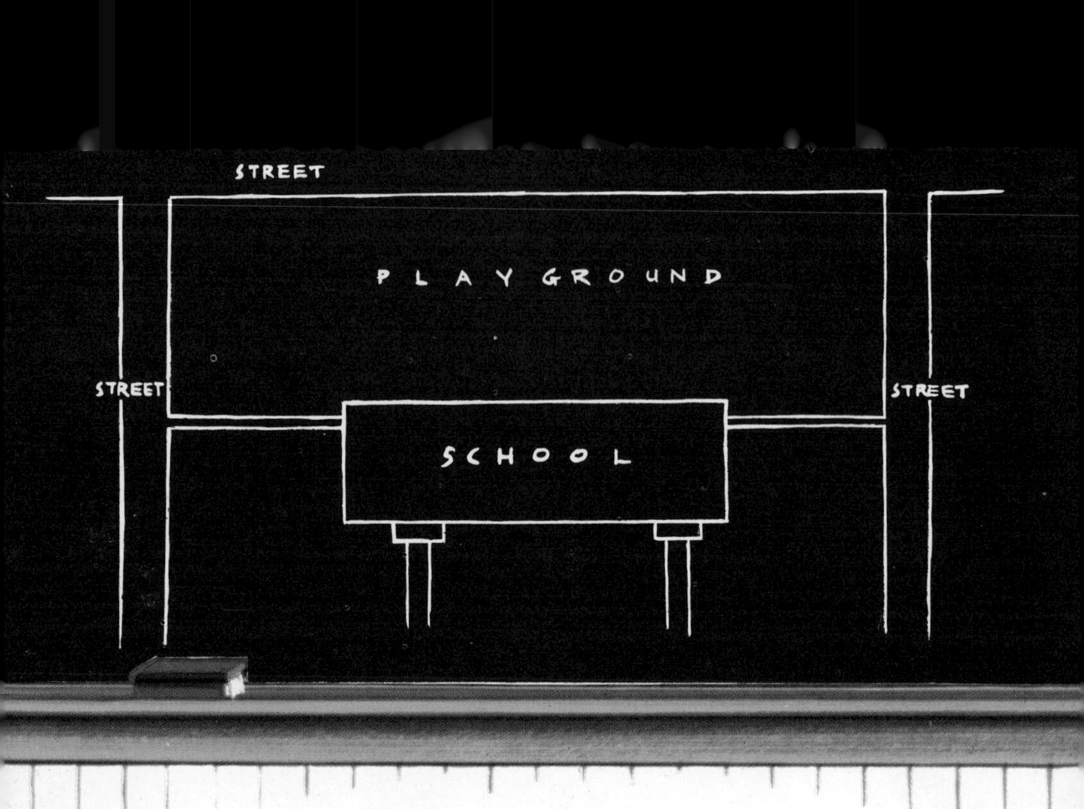

We Plan a Trip

First we talk about our trip.
We plan where to go.
Is it far or near?
We plan how to go.
Do we walk or ride?
We talk about safe ways to go.
We talk about what we want to find out.
Then we go.

We Use Wood

This truck brings wood.
The wood smells good.
It smells like a Christmas tree.
The wood was a tree.
The tree was cut.
Now the wood looks like this.
It is ready for the new building.

We Use Iron

These things are made of iron.
The iron was once in the ground.
The iron looked like soft earth.
Men dug the iron out of the ground.
Then other men made it
into many things.
Here are some things made of iron.
They are for the new building.

We Use Glass

Here is glass for the new building.

Shining glass from shining sand!

Glass is made from sand mixed with other things.

A very hot fire turns the mixture into glass.

Glass does not look like the things that it was made from.

Does a cake look like the things that it was made from?

We Use Stone

Here is stone for the new building.
This stone was once part
of a mountain.
Men cut it out of the mountain.
Now part of a mountain is part
of the building.

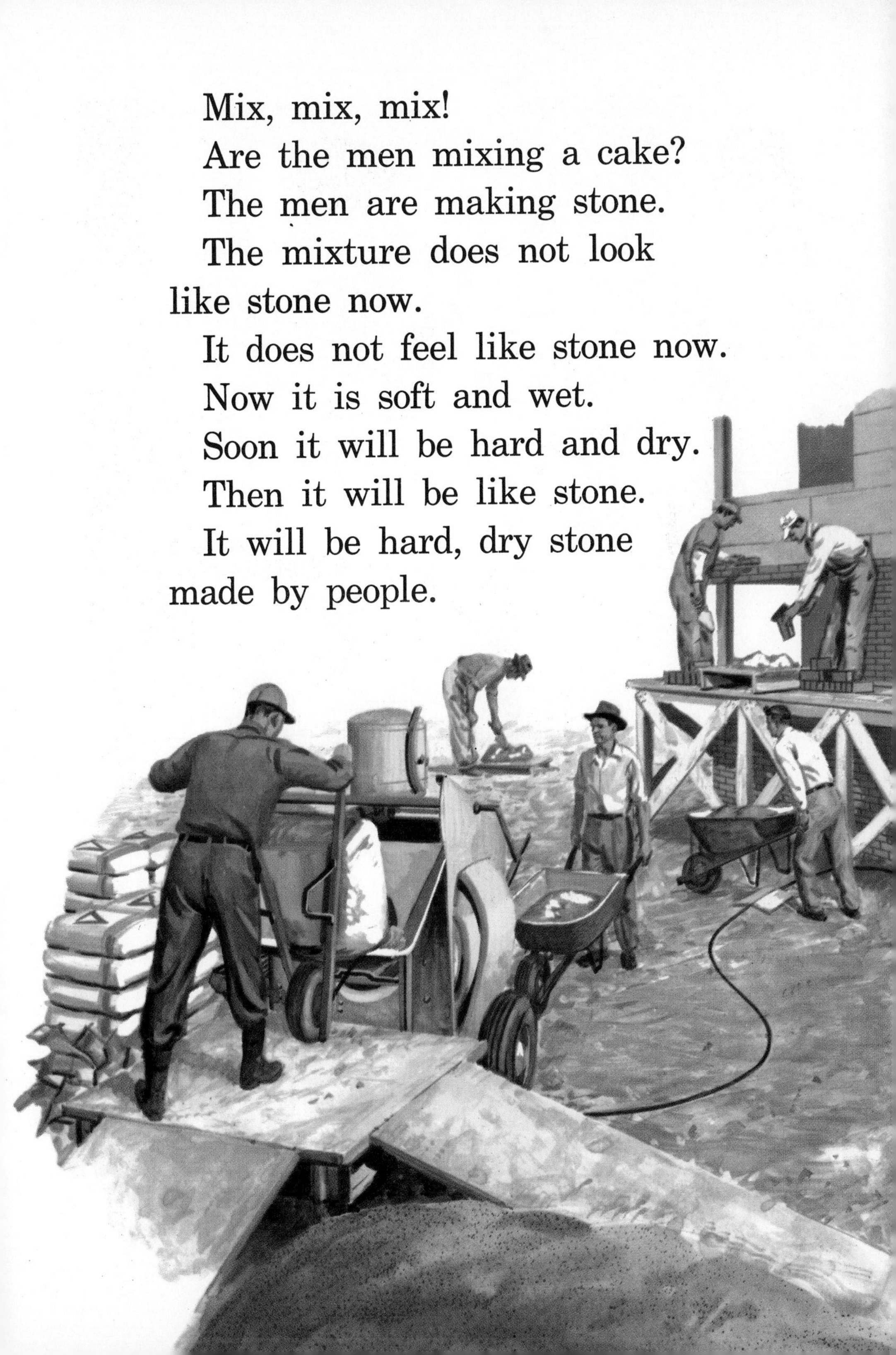

Mix, mix, mix!

Are the men mixing a cake?

The men are making stone.

The mixture does not look like stone now.

It does not feel like stone now.

Now it is soft and wet.

Soon it will be hard and dry.

Then it will be like stone.

It will be hard, dry stone made by people.

We like to mix, too.
We mix with water.
The mixture is soft and wet.
We make shapes from the mixture.
We wait for the mixture to become hard and dry.
Then it will be like stone!

Things to Talk About

1. Can you see any buildings near your school? Tell what they are made of.
2. Tell what happens in each picture.
   Which happens first?
   Which happens next?

3. Heat is used in making glass.
   Tell what heat does to these things.

Things to Do

1. Make a house book.
   Find these pictures to put in it.
   A house made of wood.
   A house made of brick.
   A house made of stone.

2. Go on a trip in the neighborhood.
   Look for things made of wood, iron, stone, and glass.

3. Bring in toy trucks.
   Tell how each truck is used.

Things to Find Out

1. Iron is a metal.
   Find out about other metals used in buildings.

2. Coins are made of metal.
   Find out about some metals used for making coins.
   How can you find out if coins rust?

3. Find out what things for buildings are made in your town.

We use many things to make
a good house.
Wood is good for some things.
Iron is good for other things.
Stone is good.
Glass is good, too.
Where is each of these things used?
We can find out.

Is Stone Strong?

Let's begin with the cellar.
Many cellar walls are made of stone.
Why is stone good for a cellar wall?
We can find out why.
The heavy house rests
on the cellar wall.
Stone is strong.
It can hold up the heavy house.

Wood and iron are strong, too.

Wood and iron can hold up heavy things.

Why do we use stone for cellars?

Is stone better than iron or wood?

We can look in a cellar to find out.

Does Stone Rust?

Cellar walls get wet when it rains.
The wet ground makes them wet.
What happens when stone gets wet?
What happens when iron gets wet?
We can find out.

EXPERIMENT

Put a stone and an iron nail in the wet ground.

Leave them for two days.

Did the stone get rusty?

Did the iron get rusty?

We find that iron gets rusty when it stays in wet ground.

We do not want rusty iron walls in our cellar.

Does Stone Rot?

Wood rots if it stays
in the wet ground a long time.
Stone does not rot.
Stone does not rust.
Stone is strong.
We will use stone
for the cellar walls.

Does Stone Burn?

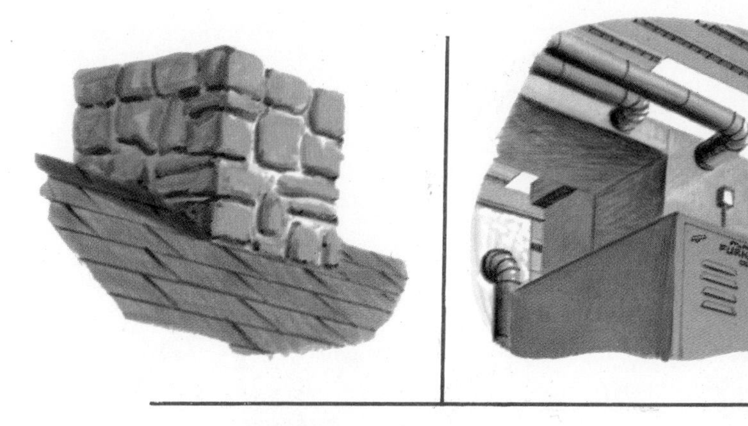

What can we use for these places?
All these places get very hot.
Some things burn when
they get very hot.
Does stone burn?

EXPERIMENT

Here is a way to find out.

Stone does not burn.

We can use stone in places that get very hot.

Different Kinds of Stone in the Building

We know that stone is strong.
We know it does not rust or rot.
We know it does not burn.
Stone is used in many parts
of the building.
Can you tell about stone
in the new building?

These children went on a trip.

They went through the school.

They found many things made of stone.

Can you tell why stone was used?

Things to Talk About

1. Tell about things made of stone that you see on your way to school.
2. Tell about stone in your home.
3. Talk about rules for fire drills.
   Tell why each fire drill rule was made.
4. Talk about fire safety in your home.
   Can you make up some fire safety rules for homes?

Things to Do

1. Go on a trip near your school.
   Look for things made of stone.
   Tell why the stone was used.
2. Make a stone road and a dirt road on the sand table.
   Load a toy truck.
   Push it back and forth many times on each road.
   What happens to the roads after the truck has gone back and forth many times?

Things to Find Out

1. Find out what the streets near your school are made of.
2. Find out what happens to a dirt road after it rains.
3. Find out how each of these helps to make roads.

WHY WE USE WOOD AND IRON

Why We Use Wood

We found that stone is good for a building.

Why do we use wood for the door?

We can find out.

Lift a brick and a piece of wood as big as the brick.

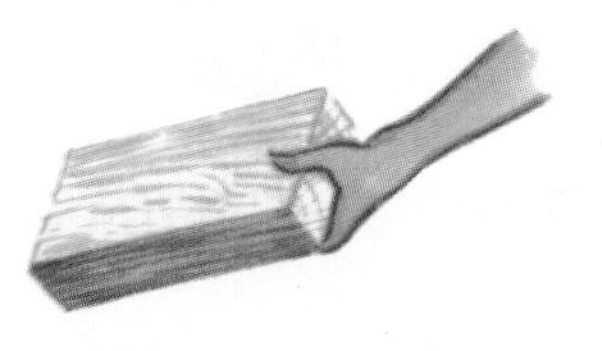

We find that wood is lighter.

A door made of stone would be very, very heavy.

The wood is not so heavy.

It is easier to carry.

It is better for doors.

It is easier to open a wood door.

You can cut stone and iron.

But it is hard work.

You can smooth stone and iron.

But it is hard work.

Is it easy to nail stone or iron?

It is easy to work with wood.
It is easier than working with stone or iron.
Wood is easy to cut.
It is easy to nail.
It is easy to smooth.

Now you know why wood is better for some things.

Wood is easy to cut.

It is easy to nail.

It is easy to smooth.

It is not so heavy as stone.

That is why many parts of the new house are made of wood.

Many parts of the school are made of wood.

We use wood in many ways.

Look around your classroom.

Find the things made of wood.

Why We Use Iron

This part of the house is iron.
Iron is strong.
Iron will not burn.
It can be made into pretty shapes.
But you know something about iron that is not good.
Iron gets rusty.
How can we keep it from getting rusty?
We can find out.

Why We Paint Iron

EXPERIMENT

Get two iron nails.
Paint one nail and let it dry.
Do not paint the other nail.
Put both nails on wet paper.
Roll them up in the wet paper.
Let them stay for a day.
What happens?
Which nail is rusty?

If we paint iron, it does not get rusty.

People did not always know this.

Then someone found out.

People have been making houses for many, many years.

They try to make good houses.

Someone finds out one thing.

Someone finds out another thing.

We make better houses because we find out more and more.

People help each other to find out.

Things to Talk About

1. Talk about the wood that is used in your home.
2. Tell the story of something made of wood. Begin with a tree.
3. Here are some things made of iron. Tell why iron is used for each one.

Things to Do

1. Get some small pieces of different kinds of wood and some sandpaper.
   Smooth the wood with the sandpaper.
   Are some kinds of wood easier to smooth with sandpaper than others?
   Try to push tacks into each piece of wood.
   Are some kinds of wood harder than others?

2. Go on a trip to a furniture store.
   Is all the furniture they sell made
   of the same kind of wood?

3. Go to a place where they cut or sell wood.
   Get small pieces of different kinds of wood.
   Put them on a chart. Label each kind.

4. Bend a paper clip into a round shape.
   Try to bend a piece of wood.
   Which is easier to bend?

Things to Find Out

1. You know why paint is used on iron.
   Is paint good for wood, too?
   Look at an old piece of wood.
   Can you find out why paint is good
   for wood, too?

2. Find out if other things keep iron
   from rusting.

3. Find out how wood was used for making
   this book.

4. Find out about some furniture made of iron.
   How is the iron furniture kept
   from rusting?

WHY WE USE GLASS

What Windows Do for Us

Here are the windows
in the new house.
When a window is closed
it keeps out wind and rain.
But it lets in light.
Light can go through glass.
Can light go through other things?
We can find out.

Light Goes Through Some Things

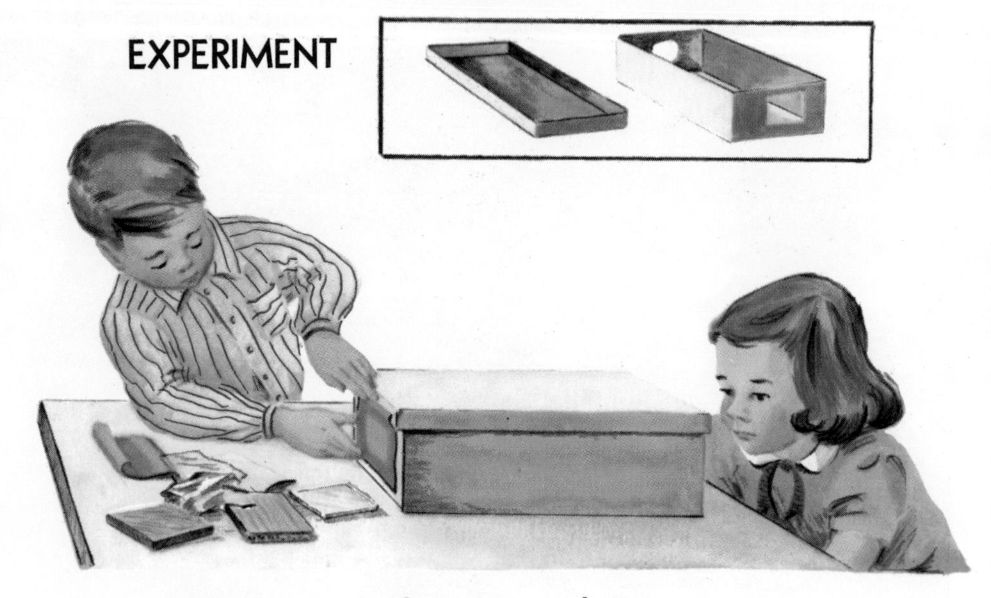

Cut two holes in a box.

Look into one hole.

Hold a piece of paper over the other hole.

Does light come through the paper?

Try many different things.

What lets light come through best?

Which things can you see through?

Can you tell why glass is very good for windows?

Glass is right for windows,
but not for cellar walls.
Stone is right for cellar walls,
but not for windows.
Wood is better for some things.
Iron is better for others.
No one thing is best for everything.

Some people are good
at making windows.

Other people are good
at making cellars.

Some people can work with wood.

Other people can work better
with iron.

Different people can do
different things.

Everybody can do something.

Things to Talk About

1. Tell how glass houses help plants to grow in winter.
2. The sun gives us light.
   What other kinds of light do we use?
3. Tell about things glass is used for.

Things to Do

1. Make a chart that shows how glass is used at home and in school.
2. You can make a rainbow with sunlight.
   Sunlight has many different colors in it.
   You cannot see the colors when they are all mixed together.
   But you can see them when they are all spread out.

   Try these three ways of making a rainbow.

Real rainbows are made when sunlight shines through water drops in the air. The water drops spread the sunlight. Glass can spread the sunlight, too.

Things to Find Out

1. Find out about good light for reading. Make pictures that show good light in the day and at night.

2. Go to a glass store.

   Find out about the strong safety glass made for cars. How is it made strong?

   Find out how big pieces of glass for store windows are carried.

   Find out how window glass is cut.

WINTER COATS

In winter some birds go away,
and some birds stay.

Other animals stay, too.

They find food, or we give them food.

They keep warm in their winter coats.

Which animals have coats of fur?

Which animals have coats
of feathers?

Fur or feathers keep them warm.

We cannot grow fur or feathers.
We cannot grow winter coats.
But we can put them on.
We wear coats made of wool.
We wear hats made of wool.
We wear many woolen things.
Why do we wear wool in winter?
We can find out.

Why We Wear Wool

EXPERIMENT

We can find out with two jars.
Put hot water in each jar.
Put a woolen sweater around one jar.
Leave the other jar as it is.
Let them stand for about two hours.

Then touch the water in each jar.
Which is warmer?
Does wool help to keep the heat in?
Now can you tell why we wear
things made of wool in cold weather?

Clothes from Wool

Many people help to make woolen clothes.

Here is the story of a woolen coat.

Tell about the people who helped
make the woolen coat.

Tell about the machines they used.

Wool from Sheep

On warm days we can take off our coats.

Sheep cannot take off their coats.

We do it for them.

We cut off their warm wool coats in the spring.

Then we make the wool into new coats for us.

The sheep grow new coats before winter comes.

Then both of us are warm.

Things to Talk About

1. Tell about some animals that
   have fur or wool.

2. Tell about some animals that
   have feathers.

3. Some animals do not have fur or feathers.
   Tell about them.

4. Tell about the things made of wool that
   you wore to school today.

Things to Do

1. Make a collection of woolen things
   and bring them to class.

2. Make a collection of many kinds of cloth.
   Put them on a chart and label them.

3. Find out how to dye cloth.
   Dye some bits of white cloth.
   Dye the bits of cloth different colors.

4. Make a collection of pictures of animals
   that live in very cold places.

5. Plan a trip to a store that sells
   woolen things.

Things to Find Out

1. Find out about animals that live in very cold places.

2. Find out about animals with fur that can live in cold water.

3. Find out about some animals that have white fur in winter.

4. Is there a zoo in your town? If there is, take a trip to the zoo. Ask to see the animals in the zoo that grow new winter coats.

5. Is there a farm near you? If there is, ask the farmer about the animals' winter coats.

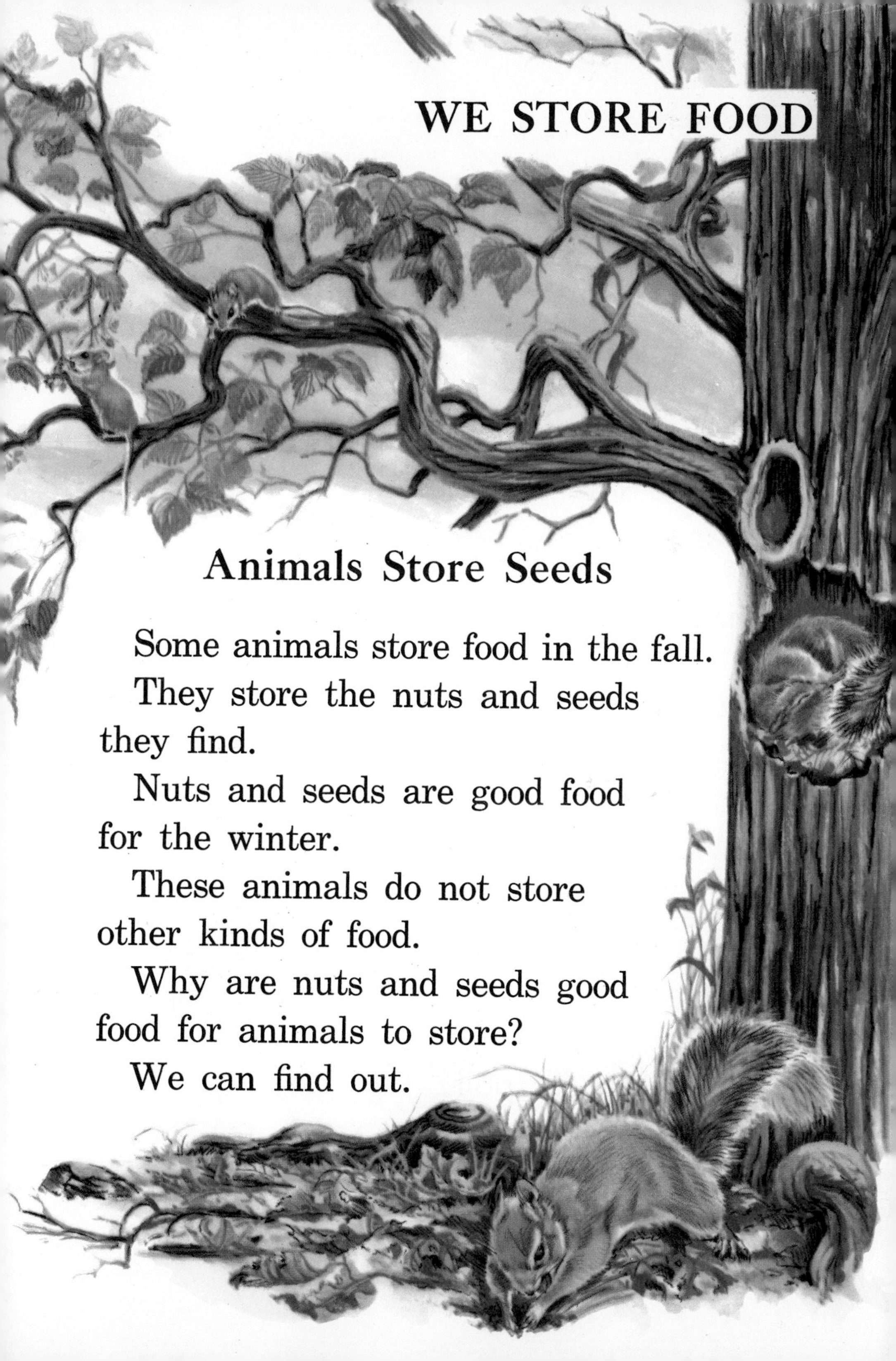

WE STORE FOOD

Animals Store Seeds

Some animals store food in the fall.

They store the nuts and seeds they find.

Nuts and seeds are good food for the winter.

These animals do not store other kinds of food.

Why are nuts and seeds good food for animals to store?

We can find out.

EXPERIMENT

Leave these foods for a few days.
Find out what happens.

Which foods spoil?
Which foods are not good to store?
Which foods are good to store?

Foods from Seeds

We make many different foods from seeds.

Here are foods from wheat seeds.

Tell about these foods.

Tell about some foods made from other seeds.

Animals store nuts and seeds.
We store nuts and seeds, too.
They are good to eat.
They do not spoil quickly.
They stay good for a long time.

We Store Many Seeds

Nuts and seeds do not spoil quickly.
They stay good for a long time.
This is good for animals.
They can store them.
It is good for us, too.
We can store them.
It is best of all for plants.
This is why.
Most plants make seeds in the fall.
Some of these seeds lie in the soil until spring.
Then they begin to grow.

We Eat Many Kinds of Foods

We eat nuts and seeds.
We eat other parts of plants, too.
We eat leaves and stems.

We eat roots.

We eat these parts of plants, too.
These are the parts that hold seeds.
They are called fruits.
They taste good.
They smell good.
Look at all the colors.

We like many foods.
We can eat many of them all year.
We know how to store them so they do not spoil.
We can store them in many ways.
Here are some ways we store food.

We Store Many Foods

Some of our food comes from plants.
Some of our food comes from animals.
We can store food from plants.
We can store food from animals, too.
We can keep it cold.
It does not spoil.
We know how to store it.
We can eat it in winter or summer.

People do not need to fly away from winter.

They know how to bring food from warm places to cold places.

They know how to make warm clothes.

They know how to make warm homes.

They know how to store food.

People know how to help each other in winter.

Things to Talk About

1. Tell about some animals that store food before winter.
2. Tell why nuts and seeds are good food for animals to store.
   Why are most other foods not good for animals to store?
   Tell about some seed foods you eat.
3. Tell about some leaves, stems, and roots that you eat.
4. Tell of some ways in which we store food.
5. Tell what would happen if seeds did not stay good until spring.

Things to Do

1. Cut open some fruits and find the seeds.
   Make pictures of the fruits.
   Show the seeds in the pictures.
2. Make pictures of roots, stems, and leaves that we eat.
3. Bring in labels from different foods.
   Tell how each food was kept from spoiling.

4. Make a plan for dinner.
   Plan some food from roots, stems, seeds, and leaves for it.

   Plan some food from animals for it.

Things to Find Out

1. How is wheat made into flour?
2. Find out about whole wheat flour.
   How is whole wheat flour different from white flour?
3. How is bread made?
4. Where did these foods come from?

WINTER BRINGS CHANGES

Animals in Winter

Winter is coming.
Animals get ready for winter.
Some go away to warmer places.
Some store food and stay.
These animals stay,
but they seem to store no food.
How will they do without food?
How will they live in the winter?
We can find out.

See how the animals get ready!
The animals are storing food.
They store it by eating and eating.
They get fat with so much eating.
The fat will be food for them.

It will be food inside when there is no food outside.

Here comes the snow!

Who is ready for the snow and ice?

Who is ready for the cold, cold winter?

These animals are ready.

They are ready in their homes in the ground.

In the fall, they ate and ate.

All winter long they will not eat.

They will not grow.

They will lie still in their homes.

Winter is a quiet time
for many animals.

They have a quiet rest
in the cold winter.

There is nothing to eat, but they
do not need to eat.

The animals rest until the spring.

Spring always comes.

I wonder, I wonder,
How animals know
To go to sleep
With the coming of snow.

I wonder, I wonder,
How animals know
To wake in the spring
With the things that grow.

School Animals in Winter

We keep these animals in our school.
They do not sleep through the cold.
We keep them warm and safe.
We give them food.
We give them homes.
We take care of them.

Farm Animals in Winter

We take care of these animals, too.
They do not store food.
The farmer feeds them.
They do not find a winter home for themselves.
The farmer gives them a home.
What does the farmer get from them?

People in Winter

We do not need to dig homes under the ground.

We know how to keep our homes warm.

We know how to keep warm in winter.

We know how to make fires.

We can burn many things
to keep us warm.

We do not need to go
to warm places to be warm.

We do not need to fly away
from the winter.

We do not need to hide
from the snow and ice.

In the cold winter our homes
are warm.

Things to Talk About

1. Who has been to a place where it does not get cold? Tell about it.

2. In the fall, some animals eat and eat. They get very fat. Tell why.

3. Which animal does not sleep through the winter? Which animals do?

Things to Do

1. Find pictures that show how houses are heated.

2. Make a winter picture. Show some animals under the ground. Show some animals that are not under the ground.

3. Plan a trip around the school. Find ways the school is kept warm. Find ways it is kept safe from fire.

Things to Find Out

1. Is one of these in your home?

2. What is burned to heat your school?
   Where does it come from?

3. What is burned to heat your home?
   Where does it come from?

4. What is used to heat the water
   in your school or home?

5. Find out about some animals
   near your home.
   What do they do in winter?

A THERMOMETER

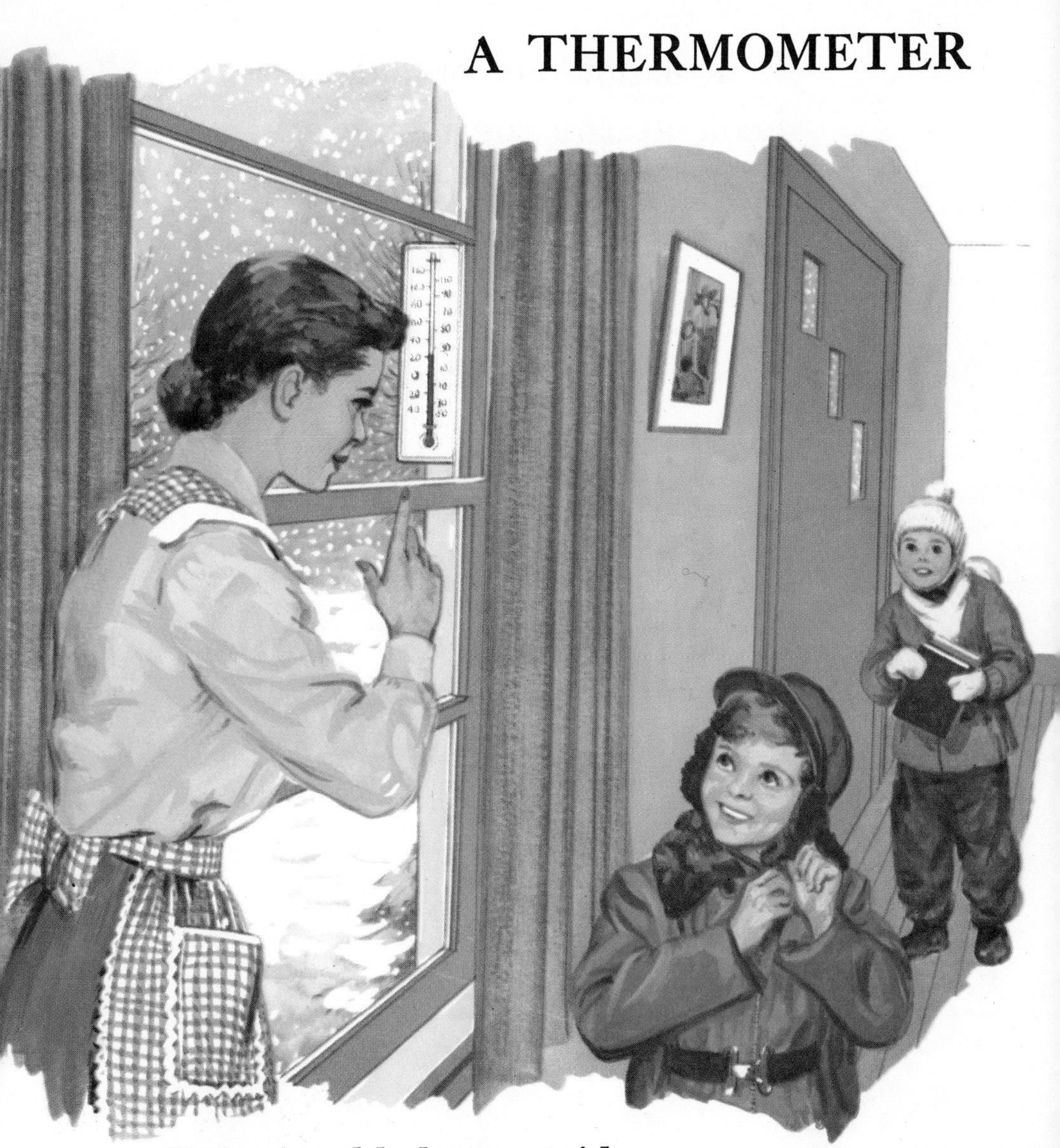

It is a cold day outside.
We will need warm clothes.
Look at the thermometer!
We can see that it is cold outside.

It is a hot day outside.
Look at the thermometer!
We can see that it is hot outside.
Let's go swimming today!

Hot or Cold

Hot or cold!

The thermometer can tell us which it is.

You can do an experiment.

You can find out how a thermometer shows hot or cold.

EXPERIMENT

First, look at a thermometer.
Find the colored line.
See how high it is in the glass.
Then get some ice.
It is cold.
We can feel it.

How can we see that it is cold?
Put the thermometer into the ice.

Now watch the line in the tube on the thermometer.

The line goes down.

Cold makes it go down.

When the thermometer touches something cold, the line goes down.

Now put warm water in the bowl.

The water is warm.

We can feel it.

How can we see that it is warm?

Put the thermometer
into the warm water.

Watch the line in the tube.

The line goes up.

When the thermometer touches
something warm, the line goes up.

What Does it Show?

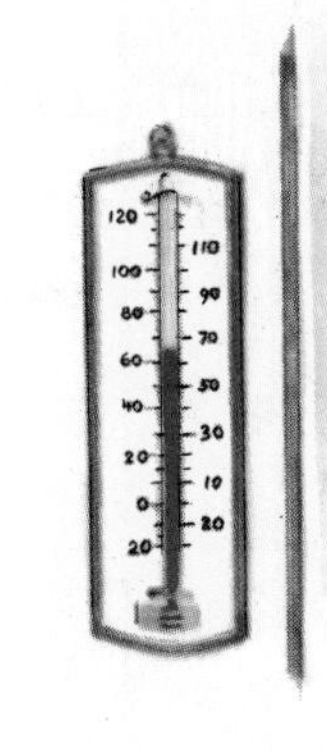

Look at a thermometer
in your classroom.
Air is touching
the thermometer.
The line is not high
and not low.
What does it tell you
about the air?
Take the thermometer
to different places.
Leave it a little while
in each place.
Are some places warmer?
Are some places cooler?

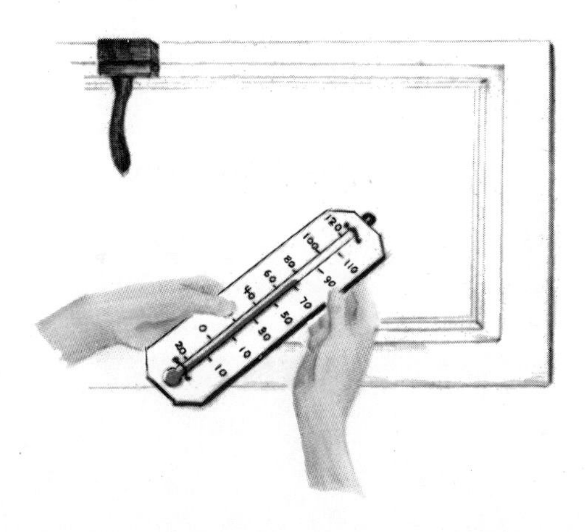

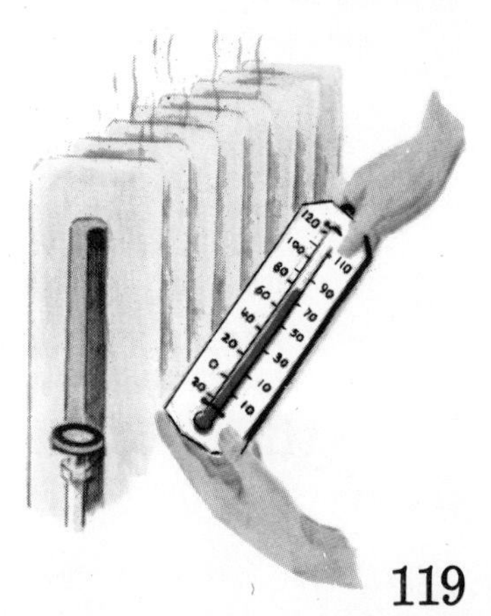

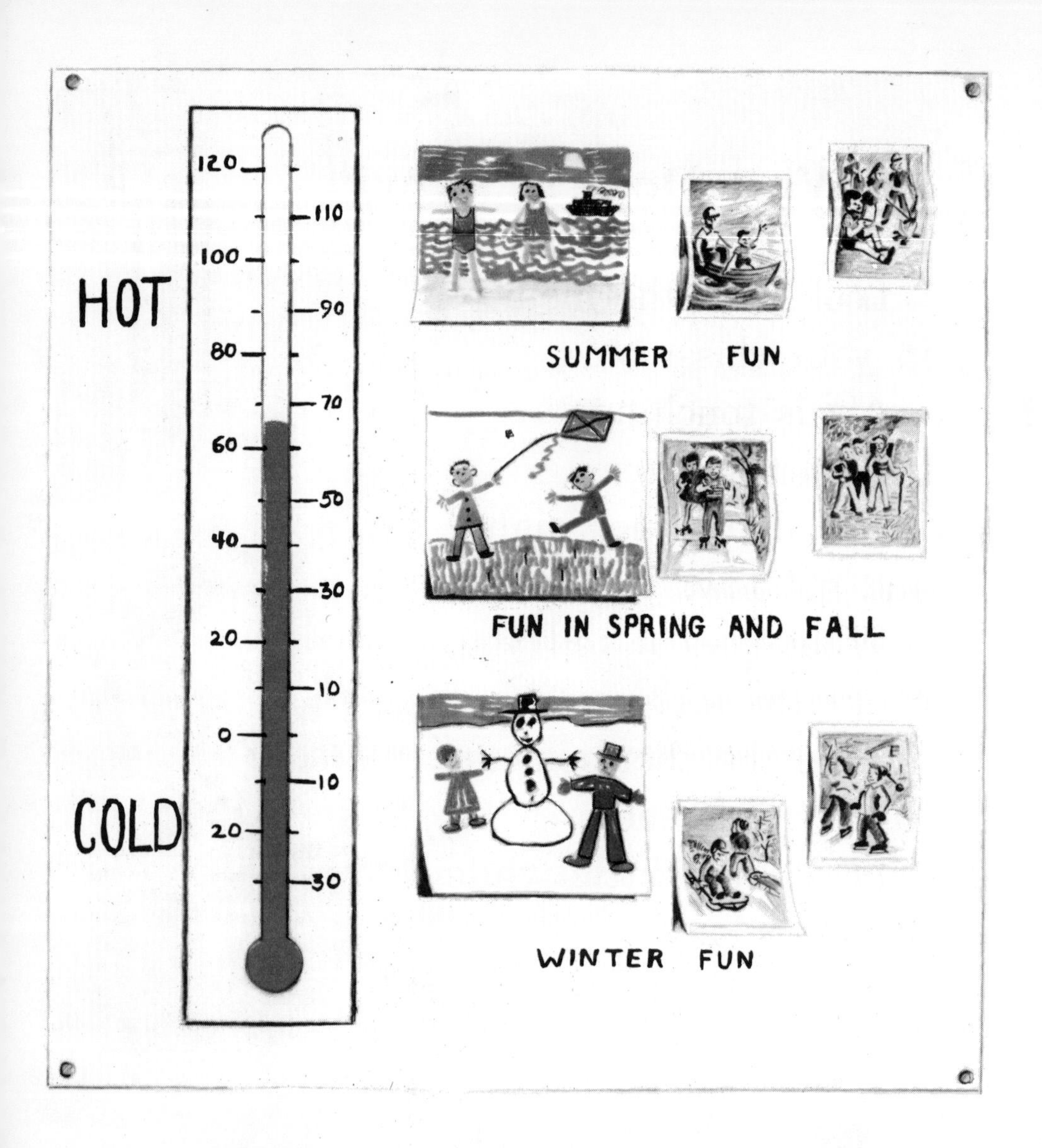

Here is a chart that some children made.

They had fun.

You can make a chart that tells things you did.

Things to Talk About

1. What does a thermometer tell us?
2. Why do we need to know about the weather?
3. Tell about the clothing you wear on hot days.
   Then tell about the clothing you wear when it is cooler.
4. Tell about the games you play in hot weather.
   Then tell about the games you play in cold weather.
5. Tell about different thermometers you know about.

Things to Do

1. Where is the air warmer in your room?
   Is it warmer high up or near the floor?
   Use a thermometer to find out.
2. Take a trip around the school.
   Find which places are warmer.
   Which are colder?

3. Draw pictures of a time you were sick and the doctor came.
   Did the doctor use a thermometer?
   What did it tell the doctor about you?

Things to Find Out

1. Here are some thermometers.
   Find out how they help.

2. Find out how you would open the windows to cool a room quickly.
   Would you open them only at the top?

PIPES IN THE HOUSE

So many pipes for the new house!
We get all mixed up
with so many pipes.
What are they all for?
Where do they all go?
Let's find out.

The pipes go into the cellar of the house.

We can tell where they come from.

We can tell where they go.

They come from under the street.

And they go up into the house.

Let's go up and see what these pipes do.

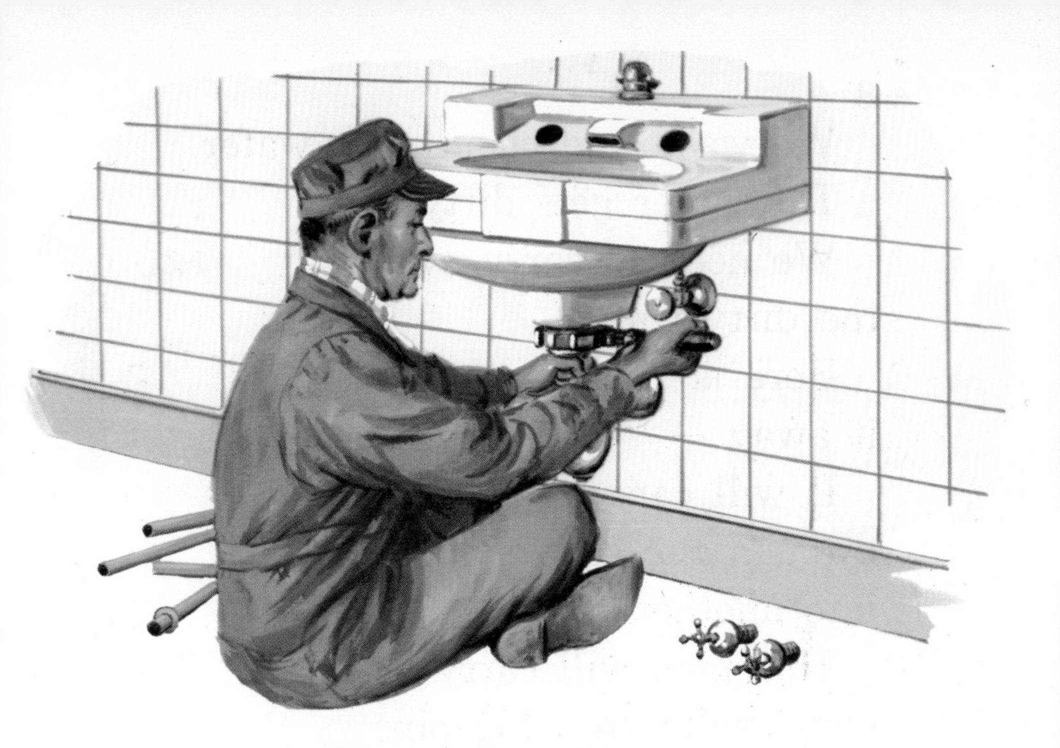

Pipes for Water

We need water in the new house.
We need water for washing,
for cooking, and for drinking.
The water comes from a big pipe
under the street.
It comes from the big pipe
into a pipe under the house.
Then water goes all
through the house in pipes.
But there are other pipes, too.
What are they for?

We wash and clean with water.
The water gets dirty.
We need to carry away the dirty water.
Here is a pipe that will carry it away.
It will carry it down through the cellar, and into another pipe.
This pipe will carry dirty water to a big pipe under the street.
Good-by, dirty water!

Pipes for Gas

Here is another pipe
for the new house.
This pipe will bring gas for cooking.
The gas comes from a big pipe
under the street.
It comes from the big pipe
into a pipe under the house.
It goes in pipes
through the new house.
Is there cooking gas in your house?
Does it come through pipes?

Pipes for Electricity

Still another pipe!

It does not look like the other pipes.

It does not carry water or gas.

It carries electricity.

The electricity goes through wires in the pipe.

We need electricity for lights.

We need it for many things.

Electricity comes from big wires in the street.

It is carried through wires all through the new house.

Things to Talk About

1. Tell how we use water at home.
2. Tell some ways we use electricity.
3. Is gas used in your town? Tell about it.

Things to Do

1. Plan a trip to the cellar.
   Find where the pipes come
   into the building.
2. Tell how these things work.

Things to Find Out

1. Look at the pictures. Which way of doing things is easier? Tell why.

   Tell about the pipes that are used.

WEATHER

Oh! What are we going to do?

The sun is not shining.

The day is not warm.

The sky is not blue.

It is a rainy day.

Oh, if we could, we would make another kind of day today!

We would make a sunny day.

Sometimes we would like to make a rainy day.

The plants need water.

The people need water.

It is hot and dry.

Sometimes we would like to have
more snow.

Oh, what fun we can have
in the snow!

We cannot make the weather we want.

We cannot make clouds come and go.

We cannot make it snow.

But we can make little bits of weather in our room.

We can find out how some weather is made.

Let's see how.

What Is a Cloud?

EXPERIMENT

Let's make a little cloud.

Put water in a kettle.

Heat it until you see a little cloud.

Hold something made of glass near the cloud, but not in it.

See the glass get wet.

How was the little cloud made?

The water was heated.

The heat made tiny bits of water go into the air.

Big clouds, too, are made
from tiny bits of water.

The water comes from many places.

The sun's heat warms the water.

Tiny bits of water go into the air.

These tiny bits are too small to see.

They look and feel like air.

But they are water just the same.

Bit by bit they go up into the air.

They come together and make drops.

Many of these drops together
make a cloud.

A cloud is made of small drops
of water in the air.

What Is Fog?

How does it feel to be
inside a cloud?
Does it feel a little wet,
or very wet?
Is it warm or cool?
Is it dark inside or can you see?
You don't have to fly up
into a cloud to find out.
You can find a cloud
near the ground.

A fog is a cloud near the ground.

In a fog there are many small drops of water.

They make it very hard to see things.

The cars get wet. The boats do, too.

When the small drops are near the ground, we call them a fog.

When the small drops are high up in the air, what do we call them?

Clouds and fog are made of small drops of water.

What Is Rain?

Clouds do not stay and stay.
Sometimes wind carries them away.
Sometimes they become cool.
When they are cool,
something happens.
You can find out what happens.
You can cool a little cloud
to find out.

EXPERIMENT

Make a cloud with a kettle.
Then put cold water in a pan.
Cold water makes the pan cold.
Now hold the cold pan
near the cloud from the kettle.
This makes the cloud cold.
See what happens when a cloud
becomes cold.

When the drops in a cloud are cooled, they come together.

They make big drops.

The big drops are heavy.

They fall down.

Drop, drop, drop, the raindrops come falling down.

You have made rain.

Now you know something about rain.
When a cloud is cooled,
its drops come together.
They make bigger drops.
Raindrops!
The raindrops fall to the ground.
They fall on your house.
They fall on the road.
They fall on the plants.
The cool water falls as rain.

What Is Snow?

Sometimes a cloud becomes very cold. Very, very cold!

The tiny bits of water in the cloud come together.

But they do not make drops.

In the cold, they make snowflakes.

Little white snowflakes and big white snowflakes!

Snowflakes in many pretty shapes!

They fall softly, this way and that way. Around and around.

They make a soft white cover on the ground.

Water Goes Up and Down

Where does the white snow go?
What is happening to the snow?
The sun is melting it.
The warm air is melting it.
The warmed snow melts and becomes water.
First the snow was tiny bits of water in the clouds.
Now it is water again.
Water covers the ground.
Water goes into the ground.
Water goes up into the air again.

Up and down, around and around,
Down from the clouds, and up
  from the ground,
The tiny drops of water go,
In clouds up high, in fog down low,
Sometimes in rain, sometimes in snow,
Good for all things that live and grow.

How We Use Water

You can show how water is good.
You can show how we use water to live and grow.

Things to Talk About

1. Tell what happens when water is heated for a long time.
2. What happens when a puddle of water dries?
   What gives the heat that dries the puddle?
3. Where does the water go after it leaves the puddle?
4. Why can't we see the water in the air?
5. A family plans a picnic. Then it starts to rain. Tell which they should do.
   Cry?
   Sit and wait for the rain to stop?
   Have other fun?
6. Tell about how we have fun with water.
7. Tell about how we have fun with snow.

Things to Do

1. Wet the blackboard and watch the water as it dries away.
   Where did the water on the blackboard go?
   Make a story about what may happen to it.

2. Make a picture that shows how water goes up and down.

3. Make pictures of different kinds of weather.
   Put people in the pictures.

Things to Find Out

1. On some days we do not see the sun. Where is it?

2. Where is the sun at night?

3. How can you find out if it may rain?

4. Find out how rain water is stored for people to use.

MAGNETS

It is fun to play with magnets!
Magnets can pick up things.
They can even pick up things
they do not touch.
Can you pick up a nail
without touching it?
A magnet can.
How does a magnet do these things?

What Magnets Do

We do not know how magnets work.
We know what they can do.
But we do not know just how they do it. No one knows.
Maybe some day we will find out.
Maybe some day you will help to find out.
But today we can have fun with magnets.
We can find out what things magnets can pick up.

EXPERIMENT

Magnets can pull some things.

But they cannot pull others.

Can a magnet pull wood?

Can a magnet pull glass?

Can a magnet pull iron?

Try many things with your magnet.

You will find that magnets pull things made of iron.

EXPERIMENT

Walk around the room with a magnet.
Touch different things with it.
Which things does the magnet pull?
Does color make a difference?
Does shape make a difference?
Does size make a difference?
What does make a difference?

A Magnet Game

Would you like to catch a fish?

We can make a fishing game with a magnet.

Make fishes out of paper.

Put a paper clip on each fish.

The paper clip has iron in it.

A magnet can pull iron.

Catch the fish with your magnet.

Can you catch a real fish with a magnet? Why not?

How Magnets Help Us

You can play games with magnets.
You can work with magnets, too.
Here is a magnet at work
picking up tacks.

The magnet will pick up
the tacks. Will it pick up the wood?

Here is a big magnet.
It will pick up big pieces of iron.
It makes the work easy.

Making a Magnet

Four children and one magnet!

Each one wants it.

We cannot cut the magnet
into four pieces.

But we can make more magnets.

We can make them out of needles
or iron nails.

Let's see how we can do it.

EXPERIMENT

Rub a needle or a nail with one end of a magnet.

Rub it one way, not back and forth.

Soon it will be a magnet.

Make more magnets this way.

These new magnets can pick up things made of iron.

They will not pull as hard as the magnet that made them.

But they will pull the same kind of things.

More Magnet Games

Make a needle into a magnet.
Then push the needle
into a piece of wood.
Put your boat on the water.
Hold one end of the magnet
near the top of the needle.
Then try the other end
of the magnet.
You will see that one end pulls
the boat to the magnet.
The other end pushes the boat away.

You can make dolls that move.
Make needle magnets into dolls.

One end of the magnet can make the dolls move to it.

One end of the magnet can make the dolls move away from it.

We do not know just why the magnets do this.

But we can have fun just the same.

A needle magnet can be fun.

It can work for us, too.

You can see it work.

EXPERIMENT

Put a small piece of wood in water.

Put a needle magnet on the wood.

The needle and the wood will turn and then stop.

Make a mark on the dish where the needle points.

Then turn the needle away and see what happens.

It comes back to the mark.

Try it again and again.

You will find that the needle points the same way every time.

A magnet needle points north.

A magnet needle that points north is called a compass.

A Compass

You made a compass with a needle and a piece of wood.

Here is another compass.

It has a magnet needle, too.

It does not look like our compass.

But it works in the same way.

It points north.

In the dark woods there are no streets.

But the man is not lost.

He knows which way is north.

When he knows north, he knows east, south, and west, too.

He can find his way.

On the water there are no streets.

There is nothing to tell the man where to go.

But he is not lost.

He knows which way to take the boat over the sea.

He has a compass.

It always points north.

When he knows north, he knows east, south, and west, too.

He can bring the boat home.

He can find his way.

Things to Talk About

1. Tell some ways that magnets help people.
2. Tell how your needle compass is different from the compass you can buy in a store.

Things to Do

1. Find north, east, south, and west out of doors and in your room.
2. Use a magnet to find iron things in your classroom.

Things to Find Out

1. Are some magnets stronger than others?

   Here is how you can find out if one magnet is stronger than another.

   Put a nail between two magnets.

   Pull each magnet.

   Which magnet keeps the nail?

   Which magnet is stronger?

ANIMAL BABIES

Animals in the Woods

Happy birthday, everything!
Happy birthday in the spring!
The woods are full of birthdays.
Spring is a birthday time
for many animal babies.
They are born in the spring.
They have all summer to eat
and grow.

Here are some new babies.
They were just born.
This is their first look
at the world.

Animals in the Desert

Out here in the sunny desert
there are many new babies, too.
There are homes between
the green desert plants.
There are homes between the stones.
Some parents feed their babies.
Some babies can feed themselves.

All the babies are hungry.
How they eat!
What things they eat!
They all eat.
They like what they eat.
It tastes right to them.
The things they eat help them grow.

Animals at the Pond

There are many babies at the pond.

They can swim when they are very little.

Could you swim when you were a baby?

A baby duck can swim.

Can a duck read this book?

So many different kinds of babies!

They all are hungry.

They all must have food so they can keep growing.

They all must have food so they can keep going.

In the quiet water of a pond,
we can find frogs' eggs in the spring.

If we keep these frogs' eggs
in pond water, maybe something will
happen inside the frogs' eggs.

Soon there may be many animal babies.

Do they look like their parents?

Animals at the Farm

Here are many animals you know.
Some animal babies look
like their parents.
Some do not.
But when they are grownups
they will all look like their parents.

There are many different animals.
They are different in some ways.
In some ways they are the same.
They all are born. They all eat.
They all become grownups
and have babies.

Babies, then grownups, then
more babies, over and over again.

The Pet Show

The children had a pet show
in their school.

They took good care of their pets.

The children gave their pets food that was good for them.

They gave them water, too.

Children can take good care of their pets.

People Grow and Change

Happy birthday, everything!
In summer, fall, winter, spring,
the world is full of birthdays.
Most animal birthdays are
in the spring.
The animal babies have all
summer to eat and grow.
But this kind of baby is born
in summer, fall, winter, or spring.

This baby does not have
to take care of itself now.

It will have time to learn many,
many things before it has
to take care of itself.

Its father and mother will feed it
until it can feed itself.

They will take care of it
for a long time.

They know how.

They like to do it.

This baby will grow and change.

Which one in this family is like you?

Tell about the other people in the family.

Tell about your birthday.

Things to Talk About

1. Tell about some babies that come
   from eggs.

2. Tell about some babies that do not have
   to feed themselves.

3. Talk about ways you have changed
   since you were very small.

4. Talk about ways any animals you know
   have changed since they were very small.

5. Tell how a baby learns to walk.

Things to Do

1. Bring something you wore
   when you were very small.

   Show it to the other children.

   Tell the children how it shows that you
   have changed since you wore it.

2. Do you have baby pictures?

   Make a picture show of you now and
   when you were a baby.

3. Make different picture books
   of animals you like.

Things to Find Out

1. Tell how these animals will change.

2. Find out about some insect pests.

3. This insect pest carries germs.
   Here is where it lays eggs.
   What can we do to stop it?

4. This insect is a pest, too.
   Find out some things we do about it.

PLANTS FOR THE NEW BUILDING

Here come more trucks
to the building.
What are the men bringing now?
It looks like soil.
But there is soil already there.
Why do the men have
to bring even more soil?
Let's go and find out.

Plants and Soil

Soil for plants!

Why do the men have to bring soil for plants?

There is soil already there!

There is sandy, yellow soil that the men had already dug up when they made the cellar.

The men are covering the yellow soil with garden soil.

Is the garden soil better?

We can get both kinds of soil and find out.

EXPERIMENT

Bring some good garden soil.
Put it in one box.
Bring some sandy, light colored soil.
Put it in the other box.
Plant grass seeds in each box
of soil.
Give them water.

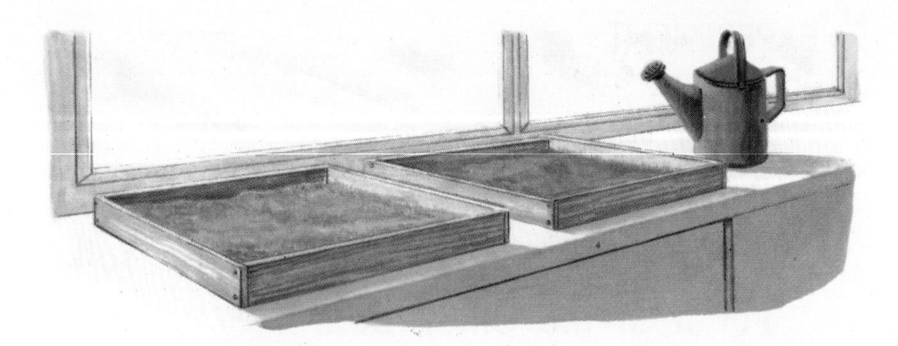

In a few days your seeds may look like this.

The grass seeds begin to grow into little grass plants.

Give them a little water.

Give them light.

Let them keep growing.

In a few more days you will see something.

What do you see?

The plants grow better
in the garden soil.

They are greener and bigger.

Plants grow better because there
are more of the things they need in
garden soil.

Now we can tell why the men put
garden soil around the new building.

Garden soil has in it more of
the things plants need.

The plants will be greener.

They will grow better.

They will make the homes
look better.

People will like to live there.

Someone dug away the good top soil here.

Plants can grow well in the top soil.

It has many of the things plants need.

Sandy soil has very few of these things.

Most plants do not grow so well in sandy soil.

What could we do to make this place a good place for plants to grow in again?

Plants and Water

Plants need water.
What would happen if they did not get water?
We can find out.

EXPERIMENT

Get two good plants of the same kind.
Water one plant, but not the other.
See what happens in a few days.

The plant needs water to grow.
It cannot live long without water.
Now water both plants.
Set the dry plant in a dish of water.
See what happens.
Maybe it will live.

Plants and Light

Plants need light, too.

What would happen if plants did not get light?

We can find out.

EXPERIMENT

Plant beans in two jars.

Cover one jar, but not the other.

Water both jars.

See what happens.

Plants need light to be healthy.

Plants and Seeds

Plants grow in many places.
Some are planted by people.
People put seeds into the ground.
They water the plants that grow from the seeds.
They take care of them.
But most plants grow without people to help them.

The plants make seeds.
The seeds fall into the soil.
The sun shines on them.
The rain falls on them.
They grow and grow.
They become parent plants.
Then the parent plants make more seeds.
What happens to these seeds?

All seeds travel.
Some drop to the ground.
Some travel on the wind.
Some travel on the water.
Some are carried by animals.
Most of them get into the soil.
Some grow into parent plants.
The parent plants make more seeds.
There are seeds, then plants,
then more seeds, over and over again.

Things to Talk About

1. What are some things that plants and animals need to be healthy?
2. How can you tell that a plant is healthy?
3. Talk about places where most of the plants were not planted by people.
4. Tell about a place where seeds have been planted by people.

Things to Do

1. Here is a way to see bean plants growing.

   You will need some beans, a glass jar, and some blotting paper.

   Put a piece of blotting paper inside a glass jar.

   Put some beans between the glass and the blotting paper.

   Keep a little water in the jar.

   Watch the beans each day and see what happens.

2. Make a collection of seeds that travel in different ways.

   Tell the other children how these seeds travel.

3. Make a class chart of these seeds.

   Draw a picture of the way each kind of seed travels.

4. Go on a trip around your neighborhood.

   Look at the plants.

   Tell which ones you think have good soil, sunlight, and water.

   Tell why you think so.

Things to Find Out

1. Find out the names of some trees that grow near your house.

2. Find out the names of the house plants that grow in your house or in the house of someone you know.

3. Find out how to take care of each of these house plants.

READY FOR DINNER!

Dinner is on the way!
Here it is in the kitchen.
It came from many places in the world.
Some of it came in boxes, cans, and jars.
The boxes, cans, and jars kept the food clean.
But some food came without any cover.
All food must be clean before we eat it.

Dirt and germs may be on the food.

We need to wash food that is not clean.

Look at the picture.

These foods need to be washed.

Can you tell why?

Clean Hands

The apples were washed.
The dish was washed.
But what about the hands?
A clean apple in dirty hands
is not a clean apple any more.
Those hands have been busy
with all kinds of work and play.
It's fun to get dirty
at work and play.
But it is not fun to eat dirt.
Dirt has germs in it.
Some germs can even make us sick.
Here is work for warm water
and soap.

Washing with soap and warm water seems like hard work.

Why can't we just wash with cold water?

Why does the water have to be warm and soapy?

Two pieces of clean cloth will tell you the answers.

EXPERIMENT

Make both pieces dirty. This should be fun for you.

Then wash one cloth in cold water and the other in warm, soapy water.

Which cloth will be cleaner?

Try it and see.

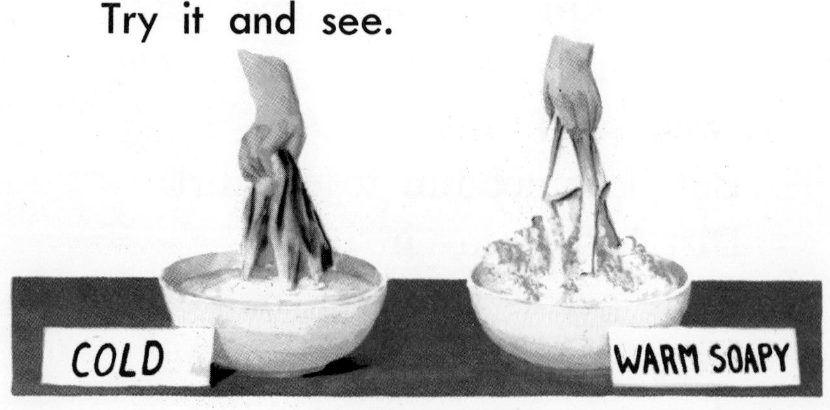

Your skin has tiny folds in it.

Dirt and germs can get into the folds of your skin.

When dirty hands touch food, germs get on it.

When we eat the food, we eat the germs.

Some germs can make us sick.

If we wash them away, they cannot make us sick.

If we wash our skin, we can wash the dirt and germs out of the folds.

Tell how warm and soapy water can help.

Getting the Food Ready

Well, here we are, ready for dinner.

We are clean, and the food is, too.

But dinner is not ready for us.

There is more work to do.

Some food must be cut into little pieces.

Some food must be cooked.

We have many tools that help us get food ready.

Tools make work easier.

Tell how we use these tools in the kitchen.

Tell how they make work easier.

Teeth that Cut, Chop, and Grind

Here is the dinner.

We used some kitchen tools to get it ready for the table.

Now we will use other tools to get it ready for us.

We will use our own tools, our teeth.

We have teeth that cut and chop.
These teeth cut and chop.

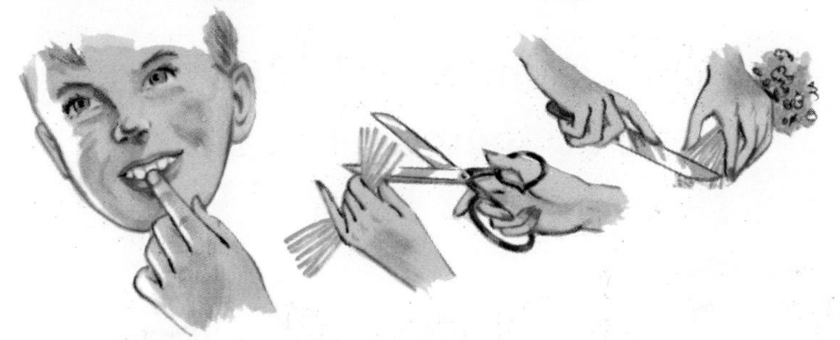

We have teeth that cut and tear.
These teeth cut and tear.

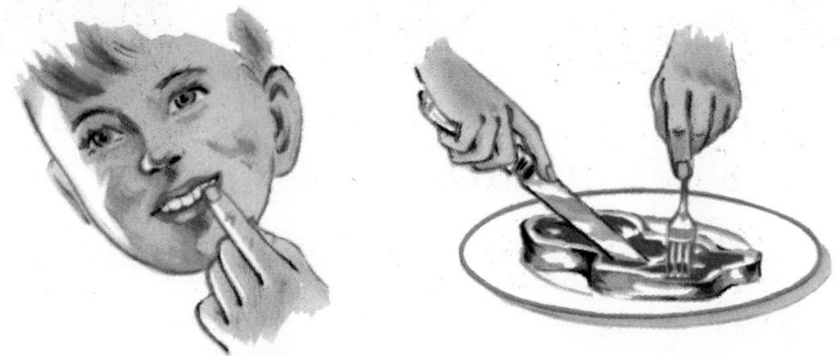

We have teeth that crush and grind.
These teeth crush and grind.

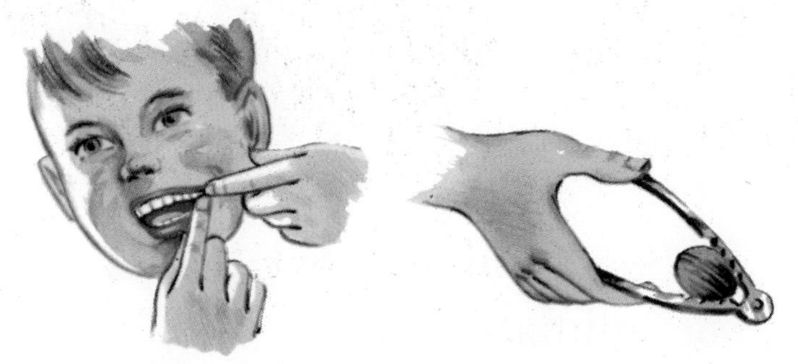

Our teeth are right for the work they do.

Animal Teeth

Some animals eat plants.
Look at their teeth!
How do they help?

Some animals eat meat.
Which are the teeth that cut and tear?

Some animals eat plants or animals.
Their teeth are right for each kind of food.

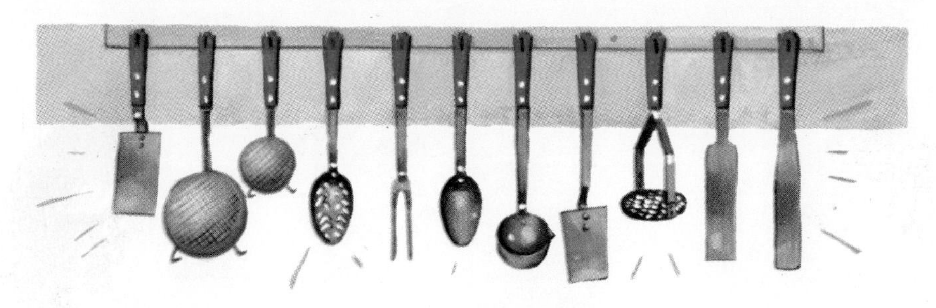

Taking Care of Our Tools

We used these kitchen tools.
Now we take care of them.
We wash them clean and bright.
We dry them to keep them from rusting.

If we take good care of them, we will have them a long time.

But how about the other tools?
Our own tools that cut, chop, crush, and grind need care, too.

If we take good care of them, we will have them a long time.

Many Different Foods

So many dishes to wash!
So many things to clean!
Why can't we eat just one kind of food?
Then there would not be so much dish washing.
Why do we eat so many kinds of food?
We need different kinds of food because they help us in different ways.

We need some foods
to help us grow.
We need some foods
to help us work and play.
We need some foods
to help us keep well.
That is why we need
different kinds of food.
Here are foods that we need.
We need some of each kind
every day.

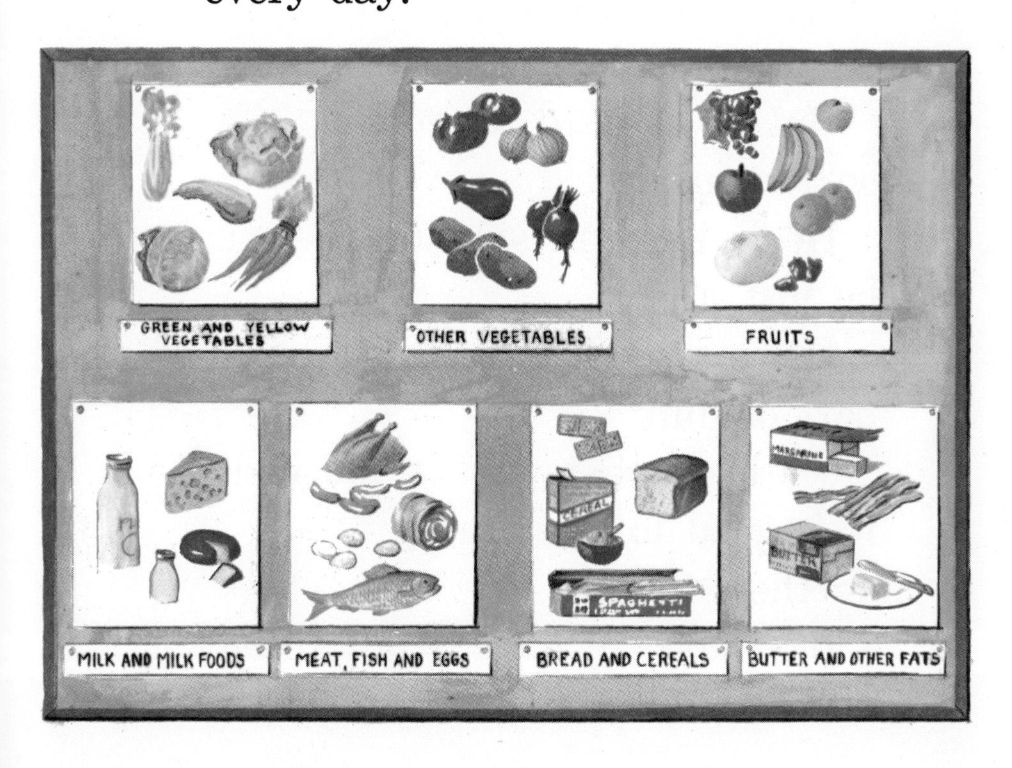

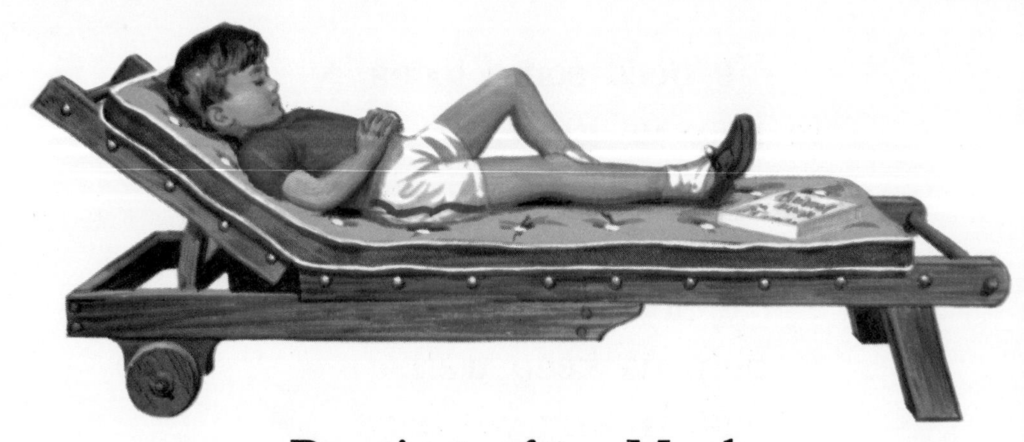

Resting after Meals

Just look at him, doing nothing!
Or is he? Look again.
He is doing nothing
on the outside.
But he is hard at work
on the inside.
He is hard at work on the meal
he just ate.
He is getting it ready to become
part of him.
With all that work to do inside,
it is good to do nothing
on the outside.
It is good to have a quiet rest
after we eat a meal.

Here are some pictures about ways of keeping well.

What can you tell about each way?

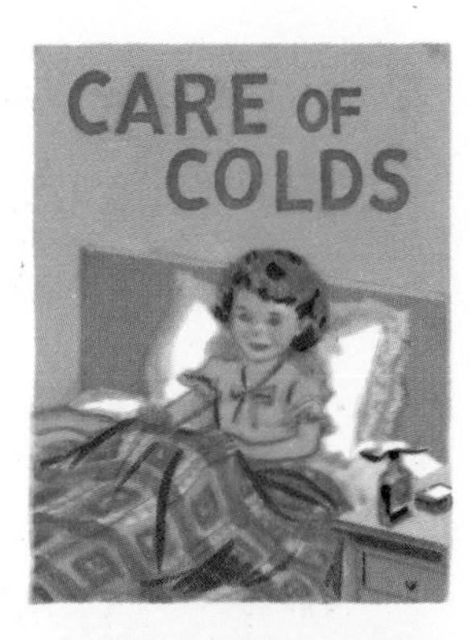

Things to Talk About

1. How does washing some foods help you stay well?
2. How does washing hands help?

   Tell about the times when we should always wash.
3. Talk about the tools used in the kitchen.
4. Tell about your teeth.

   What kinds do you have?

   Have you lost any teeth?

   Have you any new teeth in their place?

Things to Do

1. Bring in some kitchen tools.

   Tell how each one works.
2. Take a trip to a food store.

   Tell about the things you see that are used to help cut, grind, and cover the food.
3. Find out the best way to clean teeth.

4. Make a collection of soaps and tools for washing and cleaning things.

Things to Find Out

1. How much milk do you need?
2. Some foods have milk in them. Make pictures of some.
3. Some people help us keep well. Tell about some of them.
4. What must be done to each of these foods before it is ready to eat?

EVERYBODY HELPS

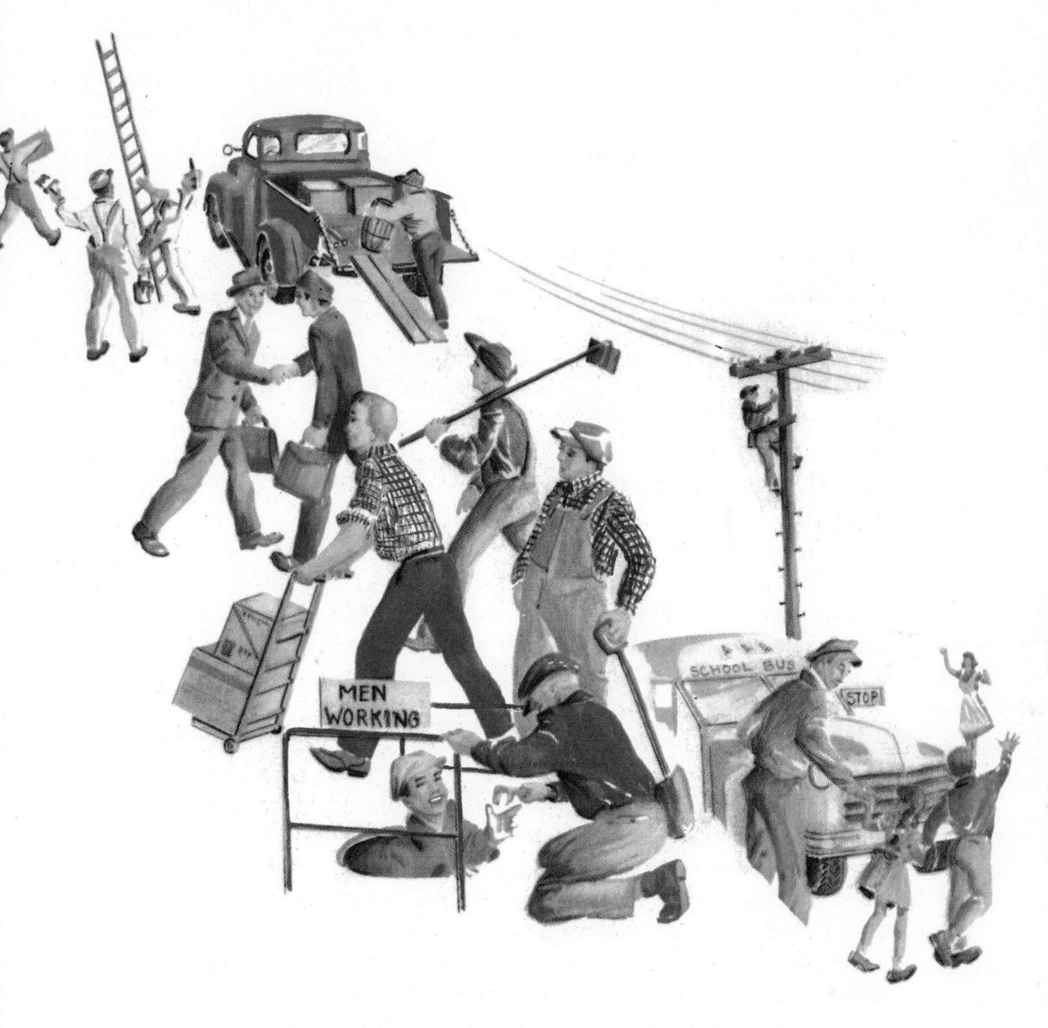

Night and day,
  the whole year round,
Outside, inside, under the ground,
All kinds of workers work for you.
Can you find their tools and tell
  what they do?

Readability Analysis

Science for Here and Now, the second book in the HEATH ELEMENTARY SCIENCE Series, meets the requirements of second grade readability.

The Spache Readability Formula for Primary Grades was used to evaluate the over-all readability of the book. This formula reveals that *Science for Here and Now* has a grade placement of 1.7, the level of a first reader, which clearly indicates that the book is well within the reading ability of second grade children.

The total vocabulary of *Science for Here and Now* is 544 words. Of these, 330 words are assumed to be known by second grade children because they were introduced in the first grade book of this series, *Science for Work and Play*, or because they were rated amongst the first 500 words of Gates' reading vocabulary for the primary grades.

The 214 new words used in *Science for Here and Now* are introduced gradually. Of the 213 pages in the book, 99 introduce no new words at all; and 92% of the remaining 114 pages introduce only 3 or fewer new words per page. The average rate of introduction of new words is less than one new word per page.

Of the 214 new words used, 98% are repeated 3 or more times. The average number of repetitions per new word is 7.6.

Of the 1405 sentences in the book, 99% contain 15 words or fewer. The average sentence length is 7.1 words.

The amount of text on each page has been carefully controlled, so that there is an average of one illustration for every 46 words. Only 11 pages in the book do not have illustrations and all of these are activity pages that come at the ends of the units.

Variants are counted as new words except for variants formed by adding the endings *s*, *'s*, *s'*, *es*, *d*, *ed*, *r*, *er*, and *ing;* or by doubling the final consonant or dropping the final *e* before adding the ending *ing*.

The 214 new words in *Science for Here and Now* are presented on the following pages. The numbers refer to the pages on which the words first occur, and the asterisks indicate the activity pages.

1 . . .
2 still
while
wash
3 cannot
softly
4 heat
sunlight
5 . . .
6 globe
side
7 . . .
8 change
sunset
9 sometimes
sunrise
10 waits
through
11 clouds
gone
12 until
*13 East
West
line
spot
blackboard
mark
same
*14 rainy
need
workers
15 heavy
easier
16 slide
drag
17 experiment
easy
rub
18 something
19 wheels
rollers
20 ramps
lift
load
maybe
21 . . .
22 building
23 . . .
24 . . .
25 note
26 . . .
*27 plan
trip
*28 class
chart
care
sell
machines
29 . . .
30 seem
31 sunny
32 covered
33 few
happened
34 lie
35 soil
36 feeding
37 . . .
38 . . .
39 travels
40 . . .
*41 weather
clothing
wear
learn
themselves
spring
park
sand
collection
*42 bean
neighbor-
hood
yesterday
43 trucks
busy
44 safe
45 . . .
46 iron
dug
47 glass
mixed
mixture
48 stone
part
mountain
49 . . .
50 become
*51 . . .
*52 brick
metal
coins
rust
53 . . .
54 strong
let's
cellar
55 . . .
56 . . .
57 nail
rusty
58 rot
59 burn
60 . . .
61 . . .
62 . . .
*63 rules
drills
safety
dirt
push
forth
*64 . . .
65 piece
66 smooth
67 . . .
68 . . .
69 classroom
70 . . .
71 . . .
72 someone
years
more
*73 sandpaper
tacks
*74 furniture
label
bend
clip
kept
75 . . .
76 . . .
77 everything
78 everybody
*79 rainbow
spread
*80 drops
carried
81 fur
feathers
82 wool
woolen
83 jars
sweater
hours
84 clothes
85 . . .
86 . . .
*87 wore
cloth
dye
bits
*88 zoo
89 . . .
90 spoil
91 wheat
92 quickly
93 most
94 stems
roots

95 fruits
96 . . .
97 . . .
98 . . .
*99 . . .
*100 flour
whole
101 without
102 fat
inside
outside
103 . . .
104 quiet
nothing
105 wonder
106 . . .
107 . . .
108 . . .
109 . . .
110 . . .
*111 . . .
*112 . . .
113 thermom-
eter
114 . . .
115 . . .
116 high
117 tube
low
118 . . .
119 cooler
120 . . .
*121 . . .
*122 sick
doctor
123 pipes
124 . . .
125 . . .
126 dirty
127 gas
128 electricity
carries
wires
*129 . . .
*130 . . .
131 . . .
132 . . .
133 . . .
134 . . .
135 kettle
136 . . .
137 fog
138 . . .
139 . . .
140 . . .
141 raindrops
142 . . .
143 snow-
flakes
144 melting
145 . . .
146 . . .
*147 puddle
dries
can't
family
should
*148 . . .
149 magnets
pick
even
150 . . .
151 . . .
152 catch
153 . . .
154 hairpins
155 . . .
156 needles
157 . . .
158 . . .
159 . . .
160 points
north
compass
161 south
162 . . .
*163 between
164 babies
happy
born
165 world
166 desert
parents
167 . . .
168 pond
169 . . .
170 frogs'
171 . . .
172 grownups
173 . . .
174 . . .
175 . . .
176 . . .
177 itself
178 . . .
*179 since
*180 insect
pests
germs
181 already
182 sandy
183 . . .
184 . . .
185 . . .
186 well
187 . . .
188 . . .
189 healthy
190 . . .
191 . . .
192 . . .
*193 blotting
*194 . . .
195 kitchen
196 . . .
197 soap
198 soapy
199 skin
folds
200 . . .
201 tools
202 teeth
chop
grind
203 tear
crush
204 . . .
205 . . .
206 . . .
207 . . .
208 meals
209 . . .
*210 . . .
*211 . . .
212 . . .
213 . . .